Lucretius

Lucretius III

A History of Motion

Thomas Nail

EDINBURGH
University Press

Edinburgh University Press is one of the leading university presses in the UK. We publish academic books and journals in our selected subject areas across the humanities and social sciences, combining cutting-edge scholarship with high editorial and production values to produce academic works of lasting importance. For more information visit our website: edinburghuniversitypress.com

Edinburgh University Press Ltd
The Tun – Holyrood Road, 12(2f) Jackson's Entry, Edinburgh EH8 8PJ

Typeset in 10.5/13pt Monotype Baskerville
by Cheshire Typesetting Ltd, Cuddington, Cheshire, and
printed and bound in Great Britain.

A CIP record for this book is available from the British Library

ISBN 978 1 4744 6423 9 (hardback)
ISBN 978 1 4744 9498 4 (webready PDF)
ISBN 978 1 4744 6424 6 (paperback)
ISBN 978 1 4744 9499 1 (epub)

Contents

A Note on the Translation and Text

All quotations and citations from *De Rerum Natura* are cited from the Latin by book and line number. For English translations of the Latin I have followed Walter Englert's translation, *Lucretius: On the Nature of Things* (Newburyport, MA: Focus Publishing, 2003), sometimes modifying it slightly, and in some cases I have left the Latin words entirely untranslated. For example, in most places I keep the Latin word *corpora* instead of using the English translation 'atom'. For the Latin text I used the online edition at the Perseus Digital Library and the Loeb edition, Carus T. Lucretius, *De Rerum Natura* (Cambridge, MA: Harvard University Press, 1992).

In my own translations and commentary I have followed P. G. Glare, *Oxford Latin Dictionary* (Oxford: Clarendon Press, 1982), and Charlton T. Lewis and Charles Short, *A Latin Dictionary: Founded on Andrews' Edition of Freund's Latin Dictionary* (Oxford: Clarendon Press, 1879).

Acknowledgements

In the publication of this book I am grateful for the extremely detailed and generous feedback given to me by my anonymous reviewers. They helped make this book better than it was. I thank the Edinburgh University Press staff who helped edit this book, and in particular Carol Macdonald, for her continued support for this project.

Many thanks to those who read the first two volumes and encouraged me to write the third. Thanks to my students and colleagues at the University of Denver who engaged in lively conversations with me about Lucretius and shared their enthusiasm and insights. The University of Denver also provided some financial support for this book.

I would like to thank my family and especially my wife, Katie, for her continued support during a difficult year of pandemic as I was completing this book.

Preface:
Death in the Time of Covid

This book marks the end of my three-volume study of Lucretius' *De Rerum Natura*. It also marks a turn in the poem to themes of death and dissipation. It also coincides with the rise of a global health crisis whose effects will likely be felt for decades.

I wrote this book during the deadly global Covid-19 pandemic of 2020. This is a dramatic but appropriate shift in context from how and where I wrote the first two volumes, which began on the beautiful summer beaches of Sullivan's Island just east of Charleston, South Carolina. The ocean wind and waves fitted the first two volumes perfectly. The island is even home to an Edgar Allan Poe archive, so that death was never entirely out of sight. Volume III, however, was written under quarantine in my home, amid the deadliest pandemic in a century.

The central themes of history and death thus weighed heavily on my mind as I read that dead bodies were overflowing the mortuaries of several cities. Authorities in Spain, England, and the United States had to store them on ice rinks instead. As I write this preface, the disease is still not fully understood but seems to have a wide range of deadly and long-term effects on the brain, lungs, and vascular system. More than half a million people have already died, and the death toll continues to rise, with more than a million expected. It remains hard to see the end of this plague.

Tens of millions of people have lost their jobs or are working in dangerous conditions. Millions may also get evicted from their homes due to the US's most significant economic depression since the 1930s. Simultaneously, civil unrest has broken out globally, especially in the US after the police murder of George Floyd and other black victims. Peaceful protests and riots have occasioned increased police violence and racist attacks across the country.

It feels like the world is unravelling just as it is in Books V and VI of Lucretius' poem. We are living through the sixth great extinction of planetary life. Those in power throughout history, and especially in late capitalism, have severely damaged the biosphere's balance. Socially, the disparity between the 1% and the rest has reached world historical levels, resulting in widespread poverty, forced migration, and death. Progress and accumulation are the narratives that justify this brutality. A long-overdue storm feels as though it is finally coming to a head and tearing everything apart.

Lucretius must have felt a similar frustration and anger in his time with the state of the world. Religious extremism, senseless wars of accumulation and greed, political power-mongering, ecological decline, poverty, murderous imperialism, institutionalised slavery, and the widespread fear of death all plagued first century BCE Rome. Of course, Lucretius denounced all this along with the progressive narratives of civilisation, domination, and accumulation that drove them. How could history have led to this? According to Lucretius, the source of his problems and ours was a deep-seated hatred of matter, motion, and death. We have misunderstood nature in the most profound way possible and caused endless misery.

In Books V and VI of *De Rerum Natura*, Lucretius flips our entire understanding of history upside down. With a simple alteration of our cosmological starting point to material indeterminacy (the swerve), Lucretius traces a whole new philosophy with consequences for virtually every area of theory and practice. Our problems are so deep that they require a radical rethinking of nature and history in the broadest sense possible. This is the focus of the present book. May the poet be our guide to a less destructive and more beautiful world.

Introduction: The Birth of Death

What is history? For Lucretius, it means something surprisingly different than we ordinarily think. We tend to think of history as a series of events caused by one another. The train of history chugs along on the stable tracks of space and time that guide it. In the most restricted sense, we often act as if only humans have 'true' histories because they are free. Nature, on the other hand, the story goes, merely follows deterministic laws.

These assumptions have led us to make some critical mistakes. Thinking that history is linear has allowed us to treat the past as absent. We often behave as if our actions have no long-term consequences. Unfortunately, thinking of history as something only humans have allows us to leave out an enormous amount of non-human agency.

In short, linear and anthropocentric thinking allows us to think that we can behave any way we like without any material consequences. However, contemporary climate change and mass extinction show us that this way of thinking about history is false and dangerous. What then *is* history? We need a better answer.

This book argues that Lucretius has a brilliant theory of history that was well ahead of its time and that we can benefit from today. This is especially the case in the present time of plagues and pandemics due in part to global climate change. I wrote this book because it's still not too late to change our understanding of history.

For instance, we increasingly realise that the history of social domination and ecological destruction haunt us in a tangible fashion that we cannot socially construct away. At the same time, we are also coming to appreciate the role of non-human agents such as carbon dioxide emissions, wind and ocean currents, and the role that plants and animals play in regulating the biosphere. The time is ripe to reconsider the materiality and movement of history.

Lucretius understood the basic principles of history two thousand years ago in a way we are only just coming to today. We still have a lot to learn, and there is no better guide I know than Lucretius.

Decline and Declination

Lucretius discusses the nature of history throughout his epic poem, *De Rerum Natura*. However, I find that Books V and VI are by far the most elegant sections of the text for extracting his philosophy of history. I want to look closely at these two books and elaborate Lucretius' unique 'kinetic' theory of history and its consequences for contemporary ethics, cosmology, physics, politics, and the arts.

Book V marks a critical turn and transformation in the poem. Books I and II began with the themes of birth and growth and focused on the role of the principles of matter in motion that must be at work for the world to look the way it does. I characterised this focus as broadly 'ontological' in my first volume, *Lucretius I: An Ontology of Motion*. In Books III and IV, the focus shifts to the perceptual world of bodies, minds, souls, dreams, emotions, images, and relationships. I characterised this broadly as 'ethics' in my second volume, *Lucretius II: An Ethics of Motion*. Of course, there is no real opposition between ontology and ethics. These are only heuristic terms to describe traditional areas of thought. In general, though, we can say that the first four books of the poem aim to show that Lucretius' material kinetic framework explains the world of things we sense.

However, Book V opens in a shockingly different way. The poet begins Book V with a series of performative contradictions about writing a history of nature. By contrast, Books I–IV expressed an attitude of relative confidence in the senses, with only a hint of complication arising in Book IV with the theory of the simulacrum. In Book IV, Lucretius argues that our perceptions are true but that our mental inferences might not be accurate because sensory images are so diverse and diffractive. The emergence of error in the senses signalled a unique shift between the first half of the poem and the second half.

In the first half, Lucretius says our senses allow us to know something about the true nature of things. However, in Book V, once we begin to infer things about the macroscopic structure of the world beyond our senses, for example, why and how the sun and moon illuminate the earth and the dynamics of other worlds, our conclusions become more speculative. The core 'ontological' principles of matter and motion, creation and destruction, dissipation and iteration are still there, but the precise empirical form of their movements cannot confidently be known.

The fact that we are material bodies situated in the *history* of a dying cosmos becomes a crucial feature of the kind of knowledge we have of nature. Our ontology and ethics become historical expressions of the universe's dissipation. Starting with Book V, we have to reconsider the arguments in previous books as distinctly *historical* claims related to the nature of our material universe and our earth. If we emerged from a material cosmos, then our knowledge is also a material process.

Human knowledge is not true everywhere and forever. Our acts of knowledge are historically situated expressions of nature's self-knowledge. Knowledge is neither objectively nor subjectively true or false, but expressive and performative. Accordingly, the world knows itself in many ways, and human knowing is only one of them. As regions of matter, we are not separate from nature, but we don't have unlimited access to the totality of nature either. There is no such totality for Lucretius. We are, like everything else, caught in the middle.

About halfway through the poem, Lucretius begins to increasingly thematise death, decline, dissipation, darkness, storms, and turbulence. He moves from things known in the clarity of the light in the first half of the poem to more dark speculative phenomena in the latter half. Book V is therefore situated deep in this darker half and leads us to the plague at Athens.

One of the core themes of Books V and VI is that material history is one of experimentations and uncertainties. Instead of the assurances of ontology and ethics found in Books I–IV, history frames the practice of inquiry and thought itself in the larger material world of speculation, decline, and error. In the first lines of Book V, Lucretius throws the whole project of knowledge into question. Knowledge must proceed step by step, by spreading out, but history will ultimately destroy it along with the world. This is not a unique limitation of human knowledge. It is the method of our dissipating and expanding cosmos. For Lucretius, the nature of things is fundamentally historical. Because we live in a historical and dissipating world, our most deep-seated ethical challenge is to overcome our fear of death. Ontology, ethics, and history are, in this way, completely intertwined.

Throughout his poem, Lucretius increasingly takes leave of the Epicurean world of rational peace and moves into the darker chthonic world of history and death. In Books V and VI, the influence of Empedocles, myth, and the Mystery religions of the ancient world show themselves in full. For Epicurus, the human mind can know the world and the static gods untouched by decay. Epicurus wanted materialism, but he also wanted a mind unsullied by matter and history. He believed in the existence of gods beyond the world and a form of reason to know those gods and find peace in their static and unperturbed being. He wanted salvation and redemption.

Lucretius, on the other hand, does not believe in any gods outside or in-between worlds. The gods are only our *ideas*. These ideas are wholly material and historical, like all knowledge. However, if knowledge is historical, it is, like history itself, experimental, fallible, and dissipative. There is no salvation.[1] This is the start of a strange new theory of history that is worth taking seriously. It throws into question the entire Western philosophical project.

Ten Brief Theses on History

At the risk of spoiling the plot of Lucretius' beautiful journey to the gates of the underworld led by his muse, I would like to try to synthesise the broad conceptual strokes of his theory of history. As a reader, I often want to have a sense of the big picture before I commit to uncovering its details. For readers like me, I provide below my own schematic summary of what I take to be the fundamental theses and consequences of Lucretius's philosophy of history.

1. *History is in motion.* History is typically understood temporally and sometimes spatially. For Lucretius, though, what we call time and space are emergent properties of matter in motion. Space and time are not the pregiven backgrounds upon which the universe moves. They have to be made, like everything else, by the indeterminate weaving movements of matter. Material history, for Lucretius, is the process of the universe's kinetic dissipation or spreading out.

2. *History is material.* For Lucretius, all of matter habitually swerves indeterminately and breaks all the mechanical laws of determinism. As such, the swerve is the source of all agency. This means that all matter has agency, not just humans. The material agencies within and around us also make us. As such, all matter is also historical.[2]

3. *History is not objective.* If all matter swerves and has agency, then there is no position in the universe from which someone can write a universal

or objective history. There is no static Archimedean point where we can get a view of the universe from the outside. History is always seen relatively from a region within history. Furthermore, recording or observing the historical unfolding of the world also has a real transformative effect on the world.

4. *History is not subjective.* Just because there is no objective view of history does not mean that history is whatever we say. No agent of history is an island. All agents relate to one another in various ways. So there are no radically unconstrained subjects independent from the world. No agent is a closed system because, for Lucretius, they are made of flows continually running through them and supporting them. Thus, there is no purely subjective view of history.

5. *The past is part of the present.* Where does the present go when it passes? If history is fundamentally temporal, then the present no longer exists when it becomes the past. However, if history is material, then the past does not disappear. Instead, it folds up within the present. The past becomes a redistributed and transformed region of the present, like the geological strata of a mountain. Similarly, our bodies are composed of past threads of old matters. If the past is material, it lives on in and around us.

6. *History is global.* We tend to think of history as the 'history of' some particular event or substance. For Lucretius, however, all of nature is entangled. Local histories cannot be isolated from the global history of the universe at large. This means that local histories are always incomplete and speculative because we do not have the whole picture of the cosmos. At one level, what appears to be causal, such as storms causing lightning, is, at the broadest level of nature, a *global transformation* of the whole of nature. In other words, Lucretius' theory of history is quite strange because it is not a linear series of causal events but rather a complete and continual transformation of the whole world. The world is never the same twice, so talking about things happening in 'the world' is not entirely accurate.

7. *History is indeterminate.* History, for Lucretius, is neither deterministic nor random, but indeterminate and habitually swerving. This means that, for Lucretius, there are no universal or inviolable laws of nature. Nature can even invent new ones. It also means that the movement of history proceeds experimentally step by step in *response to* (but not determined by) what came before. History is genuinely creative and novel, but such novelties do not emerge *ex nihilo*. Each unique event arises

relationally and iteratively concerning what happened before. This is because the past remains active and carried forward in the present.

8. *History is dissipative.* For Lucretius, our universe tends to flow and spread out from an initial high concentration to a lower level until it dissipates everything completely. Since the world was born and moves, it will eventually die. However, because the movement of matter is indeterminate, the rebirth of the world is also indeterminate. Matter could weave our world, and it remains possible for it to reweave it again, or not.

9. *History is iterative.* The universe does not unravel or dissipate itself in a perfectly uniform way. This is another consequence of the material indeterminacy of the swerve. Nature does not know in advance the most efficient way to unravel itself, so it habitually swerves to experiment. Iterative patterns such as dendrites and vortices are some of the most efficient methods of dissipating motion and energy in the universe. Therefore, as Lucretius does, we tend to see them virtually everywhere and at every scale in nature, from dust motes to storm clouds to celestial bodies. These patterns tend to emerge not because of any divine plan but because they increase dissipation and hasten the death of the cosmos. The world dissipates through iteration and iterates by dissipation.

10. *History is finite, matter is indefinite.* The universe has a history that begins with its birth and ends when it finally unravels everything woven from it into its constituent threads. The world, for Lucretius, is therefore finite. Matter, on the other hand, is indefinite or in-finite (not-finite). Matter, according to Lucretius, is neither created nor destroyed but indeterminately transformed into many worlds, all tending towards dissipation. Therefore, history is material, but matter, we could say, has an indefinite number of finite histories.

Similarly, history is indeterminate because so is matter. Even the birth of world history, for example, is an indeterminate event. There was no necessity for the world to be born.

The Art of History

The human art of history began, Lucretius says, when humans started telling stories about the world. For over a hundred thousand years, humans have been creating histories through oral storytelling. In the Western tradition, these tales circulated across the archaic world through bards who memorised sections of metered verse. Eventually, they wrote these stories down. These are the oldest records we have of archaic Greek culture.

History was, therefore, originally poetry meant to be sung and heard. This is significant for Lucretius because it means that poetry and history were initially identical. Over time, we have tended to separate knowledge into poetry, philosophy, history, etc. In doing so, however, we lost something that Lucretius wants to retrieve. *De Rerum Natura* reweaves art, science, ethics, and ontology back together in the spirit of the first epic poets.

Humans created poetic histories so that others would remember them. This is why they were composed so beautifully in order and rhythm. For most of human existence, we have told histories that also functioned as works of art. Why? The circulation of stories and truths is related to being retold by others. They live on through retelling. There is, therefore, a profoundly aesthetic dimension to knowledge and history.

Like natural histories, human histories tend to spread out through differential repetitions. They move from teller to teller through retellings that are not identical to the previous telling. Therefore, there is a beautiful resonance between the material process of history and the human art of storytelling. History ceases to be a representation and becomes performance. Both natural and human histories tend to emphasise creativity, experimentation, and beauty. Lucretius makes this point throughout Books V and VI. Even historical methods that try to emphasise reason, causality, and objectivity have an aesthetic appeal that allows them to spread out and reproduce.

Therefore, history is an art because we are always in history and have a sensuous relationship to the performance of telling it. This does not mean that we can make up any story whatever. Instead, our telling is materially responsive (not imitative) to the way the world is. In other words, by telling history, we are also enacting it and, in that way, expressing its reality. Lucretius, as we will see, fully embraces this aesthetic dimension of history in a way few others had done since the epic poets.

A Thermodynamics of the Plague

Another fascinating perspective Lucretius brings to the study of history is his dramatisation of it in the context of the plague at Athens at the end of Book VI. For most readers, this is a shocking view of history and a dark way to end the poem. For Lucretius, however, it is a crucial feature of history. History is a process of destruction and death. Dissolution makes possible new creation and vice versa. However, all the creation and destruction in the universe tends towards destruction. This is what Lucretius' description of the plague intimately drives home. There is no salvation or redemption. The process of movement takes us to the end of things and the dissolution of knowledge.

Very few readers of Lucretius have liked or wanted to affirm this radical conclusion. Yet it is a central feature of his historical materialism. One of the few who understood the importance of this idea was Karl Marx. Marx explicitly described Lucretius' view of history as a 'negative dialectic', opposed to the positive and synthetic dialectic proposed by Hegel. The materialist dialectic that Marx drew from Lucretius is not defined by developmental stages of historical progress but by the gradual process of dissipation and death. 'Thus dialectic is death', Marx writes, 'death and love are the myth of negative dialectic.'[3]

Books V and VI, with their litany of turbulence and destruction, hammer home the fundamental point that everything is unravelling. There are no gods, no forms, no essences, nor any form of salvation waiting to redeem our 'progress' or 'knowledge'. Nothing is universal. Death remains for all, even the universe.

This is also a profoundly thermodynamic insight. The French philosopher Michel Serres was the first to see this clearly in Lucretius.

> We call this the second law of thermodynamics. It was not unknown to the Greeks, at least since Heraclitus. History, or the idea of history, is only the translation or transposition of this material principle . . . Progressive civilization is only one response to time's erosion. It sails upstream in the entropic river.[4]

For Serres, thermodynamic history is the material process of cosmic dissipation from a high concentration of energy to a low one. The idea of time is an abstraction derived from a more fundamental material feature of our universe. Virtually all human error stems from our fundamental misunderstanding about the nature of *history*.

> The increasing labour of humanity seeks to halt this irrevocability. There is progress, and no progress: history advances at the surface, while it recedes at depth. It heads upstream against a current that descends more quickly than it can advance. The difference is telling, the plague will return.[5]

Just as we watch the plague painfully unravel the population of Athens bit by bit, history will unravel the world bit by bit. History is the plague of the world. Stars burn with fever then explode in a thousand pieces like the ulcerated body of the plague victim. The nature of things is no lovefest. Progress, religion, and immortality are lies that only magnify our anxiety and hatred of a moving and dying world. The challenge is to die well and without fear of what happens afterwards.

Another close reader of Lucretius, Virginia Woolf, proposed a similarly hydrodynamic image of history. For Woolf, the past is not chronologically before the present but hidden *within* the present as its immanent depth.

> The past only comes back when the present runs so smoothly that it is like the sliding surface of a deep river. Then one sees through the surface to the depths. In those moments I find one of my greatest satisfactions, not that I am thinking of the past; but that it is then that I am living most fully in the present. For the present when backed by the past is a thousand times deeper than the present when it presses so close that you can feel nothing else.[6]

When we see the past as immanently folded up in the present, this is the fullest and deepest present. In Woolf's moments of becoming, she finds great joy and pleasure not in thinking 'about the past', but in the deep past, completely saturating the present.

This is a fascinating and even ecological theory of history. If history is a river whose surface is the present and whose depth is the past, then time is not linear but rather an emergent product of the transformation of the whole river. In this model, there is no objective past state of the river to contrast with the present – since the entire surface (and depth) of the river is continually different. There is, ontologically speaking, no prior river 'state' that we can point to and say the current stream is time 2 of time 1. There is no 'common time' because there is no fixed *a priori* background that we could call nature that remains the same through its changes.

History, for Woolf, is not a series of discrete states happening on a static background but a continuously changing whole in constant flux and dissipation. The movement of the river is primary, and one discovers this in what Woolf calls 'a moment of being'. Woolf's moments are thus not discrete slices of time, either – each moment contains the deep history of the cosmos. When the river's surface is smooth, as it is in her moments, one can see straight to the bottom.

The Epicurean Hypothesis

I also would like to distinguish Lucretius' view of history from that of Epicurus. We are all told that Lucretius was a faithful student of Epicurus. Let us call this the 'Epicurean hypothesis'. This hypothesis holds so strong a sway over most interpretations of Lucretius that virtually everything in *De Rerum Natura* is assumed to have been said initially by Epicurus. Let's take an example deeply relevant to their theories of history: the swerve.[7]

Many readers, ancient, modern, and contemporary, attribute the swerve to Epicurus, despite the fact that we have no extant text from Epicurus where he mentions it. Epicurus wrote letters to Herodotus, in which he aimed to lay out his core philosophical system for students to memorise, but nowhere did he mention the swerve. His philosophy seems to function coherently without it. Not even the careful ancient biographer of philosophers, Diogenes Laertius, says that Epicurus ever wrote of it. However, other Greek-speaking ancient philosophers such as Philodemus, Diogenes of Oenoanda, Plutarch, and Simplicius say that Epicurus mentioned a swerve, or *pareklisis*.[8]

Why, then, did Epicurus not make use of the swerve in his extant writings on freedom?[9] It is possible that we may discover mention of a swerve in Epicurus' lost book *On Nature*. Yet, based on the known titles of its 37 chapters and their extant fragments, it seems more likely to me that the swerve was more fundamental, systematic, and developed in Lucretius' philosophy. This is what I have tried to show in this trilogy of books on Lucretius.

Since we have no text where Epicurus writes about the swerve, it isn't easy to know how it functioned in his philosophical system, if at all. Above all, we should not assume that it featured precisely as it does for Lucretius. Here is my informed speculation on the matter. Based on Philodemus' ascription of the term *pareklisis* to Epicurus, it seems unlikely that it *never* appeared anywhere in his writings. However, the fact that the term is missing from Epicurus' and Diogenes' accounts indicates that the swerve was in all likelihood a later addition ascribed to *human* freedom alone and not to the agency of *matter* more broadly, as it was for Lucretius.

This modest move would have secured a double win for Epicurus. Granting the soul the ability to swerve freely would have rebutted Aristotle's critique of determinism and left the core metaphysics of atomism more or less unaffected, requiring no revision. At the same time, it would have secured a foundation for Epicurus' ethics by allow-ing humans to detach themselves from suffering caused by nature. They would have then been free to contemplate the static immortal gods with their reason unaffected by matter's turbulence. I would not be surprised if this is what we discover in the ashes of book 25 of Epicurus' *On Nature*. Yet it remains puzzling why Epicurus chose not to discuss the swerve in his extant writings on human freedom in his letters to Herodotus. Perhaps the swerve was a later idea? No one knows.

The Lucretian Formula

I have spent almost a decade working on an alternative to the Epicurean hypothesis, which we might loosely call the 'Lucretian formula'. In general, I believe that Epicurus profoundly influenced Lucretius. However, I also think that Lucretius diverged from Epicurus in several significant ways. I believe these differences justify an entirely new reading and translation of Lucretius' *De Rerum Natura*. More specifically, I think they define Lucretius as a philosopher of movement and motion.

While this is not the place to reproduce my arguments in full from the other two volumes of my Lucretius project, it is still worth summarising the fundamental theses that inform my re-reading him. This is especially important for those readers who have not read the first two volumes of this trilogy.

Three Theses on Lucretius

My version of the 'Lucretian formula' has three theses. I develop each thesis through close reading, translation, and argumentation throughout all three volumes of this trilogy.

1. *No Atoms.* This is at once the most obvious and yet most outlandish thesis. Nevertheless, it must be said that Lucretius never used the Greek word *átomos* or the Latin word *atomus*. He also did not use the Latin word *particula* (particle) or any other discrete or single term to describe matter. Although no one had yet coined the word *atomus* when Lucretius wrote, it would have been just as easy for him to do so as it was for Cicero, who first used the term not long afterwards. Indeed, Cicero seems sur-prised that Lucretius had not already done so. This is especially the case because Lucretius invented many other Latin words throughout *De Rerum Natura*.

English translators have added the terms 'atom' and 'particle' to the text based on the Epicurean hypothesis. Interestingly, the only English translation of *De Rerum Natura* I am aware of which does not use the word 'atom' is the first one. Lucy Hutchinson was a seventeenth-century poet who, as a woman, was denied a university education and thus discovered Lucretius without the weight of the Epicurean hypothesis.

However, on its own, the lack of the word *atomus* in *De Rerum Natura* does not necessarily mean that Lucretius had a different philosophical system in mind. One would have to show that this simple omission hid a much deeper and systematic philosophy. This is what I tried to do in *Lucretius I: An Ontology of Motion*. I wanted to show that by bracketing the Epicurean hypothesis of atomism, there was a different yet entirely consistent theory of nature, based on flows, folds, and weaving.

Most readers have interpreted Leucippus, Democritus, and Epicurus as understanding atoms as always in motion, but fundamentally unchanged, indivisible, and thus *internally* static. But the Greek word *átomos* was an adjective that meant 'indivisible'. Readers have transliterated this word into the noun 'atom'. However, Epicurus also used the noun *soma*, meaning 'body', just as often. Perhaps matter, for Epicurus, was not quite as discrete as people think. In any case, instead of positing discrete atoms as ontologically primary, as many ancient and later modern atomist interpretations do, one of Lucretius' most significant moves was to assert the *movement or flow of matter as primary*.

2. *No Stasis*. This thesis is related to the first but has a significant consequence that distinguishes Lucretius' ethics from Epicurus. For Epicurus, there are two kinds of pleasures: *katastematic* pleasures and kinetic pleasures. *Katastematic* pleasures occur in the absence of pain (*aponia*) and a calm mind (*ataraxia*). Kinetic pleasures, however, are those that arise through movement and action. Epicurean ethics aims to attain the former and to try one's best to steer clear of the latter. For Epicurus, only the gods exist in perfect *ataraxia*.

There are, without doubt, similarities between Lucretian and Epicurean ethics, but let's focus on two critical differences. First and most importantly, Lucretius has only kinetic sensations because all of matter is in motion, including the mind. The interconnected, unceasing, and continuous movement of the mind, body, and soul is the central thesis of Book III and the subject of *Lucretius II: An Ethics of Motion*. Lucretius is also explicit in numerous places that there is nothing static in nature. The mind cannot escape movement through rational contemplation. Thus one will never find Lucretius saying, as Epicurus does, that one should try and avoid all kinetic pleasures.

Second, for Epicurus, the highest pleasure is the cessation of hunger and bodily pain. Above that, there are only qualitative differences in minimum pleasures. For Lucretius, however, art and ecstatic experiences offer great pleasures above and beyond not being hungry. Lucretius is still in favour of pleasure that will not eventually result in pain for others or oneself later on. He thinks we achieve this pleasure, however, not through contemplation but through art and sensual ecstasy.

3. *No Gods.* Epicurus believed in the transcendent existence of static and immortal gods 'between worlds' (*metakosmia*). He also worshipped them in traditional ritual practices and prayer. For Epicurus there is a region of nature that is utterly ahistorical, static, and immune to change, death, and dissipation. By knowing and contemplating this realm, Epicurus thought we could secure peace of mind beyond the material world of flux and dissipation. Our world may be mortal, but we can achieve a kind of redemption through our contemplation of that which does not die: the gods. Epicurus did not fear death because he could contemplate something that did not die.

Nothing, however, could be further from Lucretius' philosophy and practice. As I hope to show in *Lucretius III*, history is fundamental for Lucretius. In particular, I give a more nuanced account of his view of the gods in Chapter 7. Lucretius mentions the gods throughout *De Rerum Natura*, but in Books V and VI, he is explicit that they are nothing more than our ideas and that such ideas emerged at some point in human history. Indeed, the existence of gods would completely contradict Lucretius' materialist philosophy of history. The gods as transcendent immortal beings do not exist, but we see simulacra images in our imagination and dreams (5.146–55; 5.1169—82; 6.76–7). Lucretius calls them 'Divine images' [*sancto simulacra*] (6.76).

For Lucretius, the gods do not exist 'in-between' worlds, as Epicurus said. Just as Lucretius never used the word *atomus*, he also never used the Latin word *intermundia* to translate the Greek term *metakosmia*. Lucretius also explicitly says we should never participate in any religious rituals, even to contemplate the gods' perfection, as Epicurus and his followers did.[10] What would it mean then not to fear death in a radically historical ontology in which there was no Epicurean escape or redemption from death? This is a genuinely radical move in Lucretius' philosophy of history.

It is time to stop letting the Epicurean hypothesis blind us to the manifold and crucial differences between Lucretius and Epicurus. In particular, it is time we took seriously the truly radical nature of historical materialism found in Lucretius' poem, with all its consequences for contemporary life and death. This is the aim of the present work.[11]

Notes

1   'Almost every inner experience has depended upon the obsession with salvation.' Georges Bataille, *Inner Experience*, trans. Leslie Anne Boldt (Albany: State University of New York Press, 1988), 52.

2   Historical materialism was not Marx's invention, it was Lucretius', and Badiou recognises Lucretius as the most radical of all materialists. 'I would submit that my system is the most rigorously materialist in ambition that we've seen since Lucretius', he declares. Alain Badiou, 'Being by Numbers: Lauren Sedofsky Talks with Alain Badiou', *Artforum International*, 33.2 (1994): 123. See also 84–7, 118, 123–4.

3   Karl Marx and Frederick Engels, *Marx & Engels Collected Works, Volume 1: Karl Marx 1835–43 (MECW 1)* (London: Lawrence and Wishart, 1975), 498.

4   Michel Serres, *The Birth of Physics*, trans. David Webb and William Ross (Lanham, MD: Rowman and Littlefield International, 2018), 153.

5   Serres, *The Birth of Physics*, 155.

6   Virginia Woolf, *Moments of Being: Unpublished Autobiographical Writings*, ed. Jeanne Schulkind (New York: Harcourt Brace Jovanovich, 1976), 98.

7   Another notable difference between Lucretius and Epicurus was that Lucretius wrote a cultural history of humans. This is something it appears Epicurus never attempted. It is also more evidence that Lucretius was not interested in merely reproducing Epicurean doctrine. However, this has not stopped scholars and lay people alike from using *De Rerum Natura* as if it constituted direct quotations from the master.

8   Marcello Gigante, *Philodemus in Italy: The Books from Herculaneum*, trans. Dirk Obbink (Ann Arbor, MI: University of Michigan Press, 1995), 42.

9   For a nice account of indirect evidence, see Tim O'Keefe, 'Does Epicurus Need the Swerve as an *Archê* of Collisions?', *Phronesis*, 41.3 (1996): 305–17.

10 Epicurus encouraged followers to participate in religious rituals in order to strengthen their mental conception of *ataraxia*. See Kirk Summers,

'Lucretius and the Epicurean Tradition of Piety', *Classical Philology*, 90.1 (1995): 32–57.

11 This book is shorter than the second volume for the same reason the second volume was shorter than the first. Once I discuss a book-wide theme I do not repeat a similar close reading in subsequent volumes. I have made references in the notes where there is overlap with the other two volumes. My aim was to reduce redundancy so the three volumes could be read as a whole without boring the reader.

Book V

1. Making History

What is the origin of history? How was the world born such that it made possible the emergence of the earth, sky, sea, stars, sun, and moon that we know today? What are the origins of life, human beings, consciousness, and language? In short, how did we get here, and what is the meaning of it all? These are the grand questions Lucretius sets out to answer in Book V of *De Rerum Natura*.

But what could a first-century BCE Roman poet possibly have to tell us today about the history of the universe and our planet that contemporary physicists and historians do not already know? Why ask Lucretius these questions? It is true that, in some sense, we know a lot more about the material history of the universe today than we did two thousand years ago. However, one of the reasons why we know as much as we currently do *is because of Lucretius*. Much of the basic scaffolding of contemporary cosmology, physics, and history, whether scientists know it or not, was initially put forward by Lucretius. Scientists have been filling in the footnotes ever since.

The idea that the universe is unlimited and expanding in all directions was described first by Lucretius and only confirmed later experimentally by Edwin Hubble in 1924. Not even Einstein, who thought we lived in a finite block universe, got that one right. The idea that non-living matter produced living organisms that developed through evolutionary-like processes was described first by Lucretius two thousand years before Darwin. Although Darwin's terminology and empirical work were much more precise, Lucretius was a strong precursor (see Chapter 5). Lucretius was also the first to describe the phenomenon of turbulence and the first two laws of thermodynamics: conservation and entropy. He did this well before their precise mathematical formalisation in the nineteenth century.

Theories are not the same as experimental observations and mathematical formalisations. However, they can act as historical frameworks that shape observation. Lucretius' poem has served as an ongoing source of scientific inspiration for over a thousand years. Perhaps we should ask what contemporary science knows that Lucretius *did not* already describe in a more general way two thousand years ago? Lucretius and other materialists discovered an enormous amount about nature without the aid of experimental science and technology. Philosophy is not a substitute for science of course, but it is at its heart.

Unfortunately, most scientists and philosophers think they no longer need to read Lucretius. They occasionally credit his 'atomism' as a historical precursor to modern physics, but, as I said, this was a misinterpretation. Lucretius still has so much to offer us if we would only give him another chance. We have misunderstood so much of what was essential for him. Virtually every great scientist, philosopher, and poet for over a thousand years read Lucretius and scribbled in the margins of his celebrated poem. Today, hardly anyone reads him. Each prior generation of readers drew new insights from his work and tested them out with the tools of their times. We seem to have stalled today. Why? Antiquity in general, and Lucretius in particular, is not a cold dead relic held hostage by prior interpretations. It is a living history for us just as much as it was for our predecessors.

We still have unsolved problems. In particular, several perennial questions continue to haunt science and philosophy that Lucretius can help us answer. What are the origins of the universe and the nature of history? What are the origins of life and the nature of human consciousness? Lucretius does not have the kind of empirical answers to these questions that we might want today. However, he does have a surprising and beautiful vision of nature that can help guide and inspire our experimental and theoretical inquiries. It requires a bit of careful reading, a smidge of Latin translation, and a dose of fresh interpretation, but I hope I can show you that this vision *does exist*.

Speaking of Nature

The aim of Book V of *De Rerum Natura* is to provide a materialist history of nature. This is no small task. One of the trickiest aspects of such an endeavour is that *we* are also the nature that we are describing. We poets and readers are an active part of the history we are putting into words. Any answer to the origins of the universe, life, and consciousness is also part of the world.

There is no position outside the world from which to ask about its nature and origins. This means that we cannot give a completely 'true' objective account nor a completely 'false' subjective one. In Lucretius' naturalism, there is no sharp division between subject and object. So what then is the epistemic authority of a poem about the nature of things? Lucretius is entirely aware of this predicament as he clarifies in the opening lines of Book V (5.1–6).

Quis potis est dignum pollenti pectore carmen
condere pro rerum maiestate hisque repertis?
quisve valet verbis tantum qui fingere laudes
pro meritis eius possit qui talia nobis
pectore parta suo quaesitaque praemia liquit?
nemo, ut opinor, erit mortali corpore cretus.

Who is able with strength of mind to compose a poem
worthy of the majesty of things and these discoveries?
Or who is so powerful with words that he is able to fashion praises
matching the merits of the one who left behind for us
such prizes, sought out and obtained by his mind?
There will be no one, I think, born of mortal body.

Who could sing a poem *about* the nature of things *composed of* natural things? How can any arrangement of sounds possibly do justice to the grandeur of nature or even Epicurus' merits, who left us the beginnings of a radical naturalism? According to Lucretius, no one born of a mortal body could sing such a poem. With these lines, Lucretius stages the first of two *performative contradictions*.

Lucretius says that no mortal could write a poem worthy of the majesty of nature or the praise of Epicurus, and yet *this is precisely what he is doing*. What a strange and provocative way to begin a history of the universe. Our first impulse is to interpret this as modesty. However, Lucretius also claimed in Book I, and again in the opening of Book IV, that his poem is so remarkable because it is the first poem of philosophical materialism (1.926–7; 4.1–2). He claims that no mortal can sing of the majesty of nature but that he has done precisely that. Should we take Lucretius' poem as a true account of nature or treat it as a false one?

If no mortal can sing such a song, but Lucretius is singing it, does that mean he is not mortal? Of course not. That would contradict his entire philosophy. However, if his song is false, then why is he singing it, and why is he falsely praising Epicurus and boasting to be the first to sing the poem?

However, another interpretation is possible. Part of the Greek satirical and Bacchic tradition that Lucretius invokes here and elsewhere (3.1–25) involved acts of self-abasement and performative contradiction to overcome the dualism between truth and falsity.[1] In other words, Lucretius' performative contradiction challenges the rationalist assumption, shared by Epicurus and most ancient philosophers, that knowledge is composed of true or false propositional statements. Against the classical opposition between philosophy as true propositions and poetry as false semblances, Lucretius, the philosophical poet, proposes a third way. What is this way, and what are the consequences of it for his materialist theory of history?

For Lucretius, philosophical poetry is neither true nor false but *performative, iterative, and expressive*. This is crucial. If we accept that humans are not outside nature, then our knowledge and words are also nature. If there is nothing but nature, then there is no place for falsity. If nature cannot be false to itself, then humans cannot be false either. Lucretius argued that 'all perceptions are true' quite eloquently in Book IV (4.216–822).[2]

The deeply felt premise of all propositional theories of knowledge is that human minds are somehow separate from nature. In this way, they can be false or true about some objective state of nature. For Lucretius, though, even error and falsity are real material expressions of nature and, in that sense, *performatively true*. Even when we anticipate events that do not happen, *inferring* itself is still real, true, and natural. If nature is wholly material, then we need a material theory of truth, distinct from idealist and propositional theories.

A performative contradiction is a great way to highlight the truth of the speech act itself. A classic example of this is the 'liar's paradox', which occurs if I say, 'this statement is false'. If the statement is true, then it is false. If the statement is false, then it is true. The importance of this paradox, in my view, is that it highlights the materiality of the speaking activity. It shows that the 'truth' of the statement's performance is different from propositional truths, linguistic references, or representations. A statement is an ordered series of sounds and gestures.

Lucretius uses the Latin word *fingere* here to capture precisely this in his question, 'who is so powerful with words that he is able to fashion [*fingere*] praises?' (5.3). The Latin word *fingere* means 'to fabricate' but also to 'feign or deceive'. Lucretius is, therefore, implicitly suggesting that he may be fabricating *and* feigning his praise of Epicurus. This is not the first time he has implied this. He said the same thing about his admiration for Epicurus in the opening lines of Book III (3.3–6).

The point is this: before starting his inquiry into world history, Lucretius is making a methodological statement about his position *inside history*. His poem is not an objectively 'true' view of the world from outside it. Nor is his poem a 'false' picture pulled from his poetic imagination. The history of the world is only possible because Lucretius is also a body in and of the world. His account is neither objective nor subjective but is a historical *expression* of nature. The world of nature he describes is not something outside him but is an immanent history that moves through him. It is not a universal history but a history of the unfolding present.

Philosophical poetry does not *represent* natural history but continues it by other means. The weaving of letters into a poem is one aspect of nature's weaving of matter into things. Therefore, Lucretius' poem is both creative and deceptive [*fingere*], just like his relationship to Epicurus. In Books III (3.3–6) and V (5.55–60), Lucretius says that he walks in Epicurus' footsteps. But in walking over the steps left by Epicurus, Lucretius creatively modifies them. Lucretius is a follower of Epicurus in the sense that he 'comes after' him along the path of philosophical materialism, but not in the sense of being an imperfect poetic copy of the rationalist original. Such an interpretation only further entrenches the great divide between philosophy and poetry, whereas Lucretius' effort was to bring them back together. One is not secondary to the other.

Our Lord, Epicurus

This brings us to to the second performative contradiction in the opening lines of Book V. Lucretius claims that Epicurus was a god. I could forgive the reader for missing the first performative contradiction of Lucretius' methodological 'creative deception' [*fingere*] (5.3), but this next one is over the top (5.7–12).

nam si, ut ipsa petit maiestas cognita rerum,
dicendum est, deus ille fuit, deus, inclute Memmi,
qui princeps vitae rationem invenit eam quae
nunc appellatur sapientia, quique per artem

fluctibus e tantis vitam tantisque tenebris
in tam tranquillo et tam clara luce locavit.

For if we must speak as the majesty of things now
known to us demands, he was a god, a god, illustrious Memmius,
who was the first one to discover this system of life which
now is called wisdom and who by his scientific method
rescued life from such great waves and such great darkness
and situated it in such calm waters and such clear light.

Epicurus believed in the gods, but he also thought that they were
utterly *indifferent* to human beings. If Epicurus was a god, it follows that
he would have been, by his definition, utterly indifferent to the cares of
mortals. Yet this is not what Lucretius attributes to him. If the rejection
of the gods and the concern for human enjoyment is something that
Lucretius claims is a primary ethical aspect of poetic materialism, how
can he say that Epicurus was a god? Perhaps this is a subtle critique
of Epicurus' rationalist approach to ethics to which Lucretius sees his
work as a poetic alternative? Additionally, Lucretius is explicit that we
should not worship or fear the gods in any way, and here he is praising
a 'god'.

What are we to make of this apparent contradiction? Let's stop and
consider the opening lines of *De Rerum Natura* and Lucretius' similarly
paradoxical-sounding invocation of Venus. Why would Lucretius begin
a book of atheistic materialism by invoking a goddess? Furthermore,
why does he invoke goddesses and gods regularly throughout his entire
poem? The answer is that Lucretius draws fabulous inspiration from
mythology, but he also interprets the myths as fully immanent aspects
of nature that can shed light on material reality. Lucretius does not
abandon mythology but instead treats it as a poetic naturalism. The gods
are just names of natural processes and nothing beyond that.[3] However,
Epicurus rejected both mythology and poetry as having any bearing
on the true nature of things. This is the unspoken tension beneath
Lucretius; praise of Epicurus and the subtext for perhaps the strangest
tribute to Epicurus in the whole of *De Rerum Natura*.

Like Epicurus, contemporary science feels the need to distinguish
itself from myth, poetry, and religion in favour of hard-nosed rationalism. For Lucretius, however, nature is nothing but flows of swerving
matter. Everything that these flows *create* is a poetic expression or parody

of the processes. Nature iterates itself in many forms. 'Nature parodies itself', as the French philosopher George Bataille said.[4]

For example, the terms 'molecule', 'organism', 'phylum', 'society' are not ontologically separate kinds of things. They are aspects, faces, or scales of material processes. They are nature masquerading as this or that 'thing', which matter flows through for a while. Drawing the lines between things and coordinating them with one another is a creative and performative act. Names are not just labels on boxes. They have real consequences that shape natural history. Speech, too, is nature.

Therefore, science has an art, poetry, and mythology that it often denies. By mixing science, philosophy, poetry, and mythology Lucretius reminds every generation that reads him that these disciplines were not always so divided. The division of knowledge into disciplines was a historical error that continues to haunt us.

So, by calling Epicurus a god, Lucretius performs an interesting *detournement* of philosophical rationalism and poetic mythology at the same time. Epicurean rationalism essentially rejected the gods' power so that humans could become like gods themselves: calm, reserved, static, and free from desires. Lucretius is possibly making a critical jab at rationalist materialism for being a continuation of idealism and salvation by another name. Rationalists have replaced the knowledge of *god* with the knowledge of *matter*.

Going with the Flow

The most important discovery of all, for Lucretius, is that nature is nothing but material flows that tend to spread out through the universe iteratively. This is history. Humans are not cut off from these natural flows or at the whim of divine judgement. We also flow.

This is the crucial contribution that Lucretius' kinetic materialism makes to the mythopoetic structure established by Ceres (Demeter) and Liber (Dionysus) (5.13–21). Ceres, Liber, and Libera (Persephone) were the 'Aventine cult Triad'. They were figures of iterative metamorphosis who cycle through a process of creation and destruction. This basic triad has deep roots in prehistoric religion and expresses a general process found at every level of nature for Lucretius. We should not think of Ceres and Liber as merely grain and wine. Nature forms iterative habits and patterns in seasons, flowers, human development, and celestial motions. Lucretius invokes the great mother/daughter, son/lover, and

Figure 1.1 Persephone, Triptolemos, and Demeter, on a marble bas-relief from Eleusis, 440–430 BC. Wikimedia Commons.

the process of 'rhythmic iteration' [*certo tempore*] throughout Book V. In short, Lucretius naturalises the Ceres and Liber cycle but also makes an essential addition to them: *dissipation*.

Lucretius worries that people are worshipping these gods through a closed system of reward and punishment.[5] For Lucretius, the world was born, will die, and is unlimited. It is not a closed circle, cycle, or 'dark' system to be feared. The original purpose of the Mystery cults at Eleusis and Samothrace, where Ceres, Liber, and Libera were active, was not to be afraid of death or the gods. There was no strict doctrine that one had to believe while participating in the Mystery. Instead, there was a secret vision that initiates *underwent* by fasting and drinking the *kykeon* or 'mixture' that let them experience what Demeter herself suffered in Persephone's death and the birth of Dionysus.

By adding dissipation to the cycle of creation and destruction, Lucretius offers us the sweet solace of mortality without fear of the gods or any transcendence. Grain and wine are fabulous, but if we do not understand Ceres and Liber as broader processes of creation, destruction, and dissipation in nature, then we are utterly lost and trapped in the 'darkness' (5.11) with all our fears of death and gods (5.18–21).

at bene non poterat sine puro pectore vivi;
quo magis hic merito nobis deus esse videtur
ex quo nunc etiam per magnas didita gentis
dulcia permulcent animos solacia vitae.

But it was not possible to live well without a pure heart/mind,
so that more deservedly he appears to be a god to us,
from whom even now the sweet solace of life
is spread throughout great peoples and soothes their physical soul.

Epicurus' description of a natural world where humans are free from divine punishment was a breath of fresh air for humanity. However, this is also where Lucretius presents his interpretation of Epicurus' contribution and emphasises all its *poetic* aspects.

Lucretius says that the discovery of naturalism was 'sweet' (5.21), like poetry. Is the sweetness of knowledge integral to its effect on the body and physical soul? Is the solace of naturalism purely rational? Is it enough to mentally contemplate that we are nature, free from divine judgement, or does the sweetness and enjoyment of this knowledge also play a role in the 'spread' and 'soothing' action of the idea? If the soul is material like nature, then the sweetness and smoothness of the uttered words must undoubtedly have some effect.

This is, of course, Lucretius' method of using poetry as Dionysian honey around the cup of bitter wisdom. Wormwood or *Artemisia absinthium* was used by the ancients as a purgative, diuretic, and named after the goddess Artemis, the goddess of childbirth, for its labour-inducing qualities. It was known as a herb that got things to flow when they got stuck, even when it was bittersweet to let go. Birth and death in the ancient world often went hand in hand. Nature is the process whereby something new comes into being when something else dies. *Natura* should not be understood as a static noun, but the *-ura* suffix in Latin is participial (the regular suffix of the future active participle), and so should draw our attention to nature as a process of 'coming into being', rather than as a 'thing'.

The honey, though, is not just the inactive supplement of this *pharmakon*. For Lucretius, knowledge is not merely a matter of true propositions but includes the sweet and soothing processes that *spread* through the world as desire, enjoyment, and dissipation. The material practice of knowledge and its pleasure, the 'will to know', is not separate from natural history.

Lucretius' praise for Epicurus is, therefore, subtle and a bit satirical. Against Epicurus' explicit disdain for poetry, Lucretius praises him as a great poet whose *sweet words soothe our bodily souls*. Lucretius then praises Epicurus as a great *weaver of words* [*dicta suerit*] (5.53) on a par with the gods. In lines 5.52–4 he writes,

> *cum bene praesertim multa ac divinitus ipsis*
> *immortalibu' de divis dare dicta suerit*
> *atque omnem rerum naturam pandere dictis.*

> Especially since he was accustomed to weave many words
> well and in a godlike way about the immortal gods themselves
> and to unfold the whole nature of things with words.

It is difficult not to read these lines as veiled praise of Lucretius himself. Archaic and ancient poetry has long been described as an act of weaving/sewing and associated with god-like creation. Epicurus was not a poet and would have seen this kind of praise as completely missing the point. For Epicurus, the purpose of philosophy was not to 'weave sweet words' or to have one's soul penetrated by the 'sharp thyrsus' of Bacchus

(1.921–6). The point was to espouse the right ideas about nature in clear propositional terms. Lucretius knew this, of course, but loves to empha-sise, throughout his poetry, his deep 'desire' (3.5) for Epicurus' 'golden words' (3.12), and how they bring on a cosmic 'rapture' (3.28–30) so powerful that it leaves the poet shaking with pleasure. Epicureans must admit that nothing could be less Epicurean than this kind of poetic ecstasy and Bacchanalian exaltation. In contrast to Epicurus' asceticism, we have Lucretius' ecstasy.

So, in yet another brilliant double gesture, these lines are backhanded compliments to philosophers for not being good enough weavers, and to poets for giving too much credit to the gods when words too can weave the world. There is a common Latin idiom *verba dare* (which is formally similar to *dare dicta*), which suggests 'to fool, deceive, hoodwink' some-body 'about' (*de*) something. Could this connotation be fleetingly felt here in Epicurus' description 'about' the immortal gods?[6] By making Epicurus into a god, Lucretius creates an opportunity to heap his satiri-cal praises on philosophy and poetry. All this aims at moving us towards a new materialism and naturalism that would bring philosophy and poetry back together again.

An Immanent History of the World

But what do these performative contradictions and satiric praises tell us about the nature of history? They tell us that the world's history is an immanent one said from *inside the world* and not a universal history from outside. The gods do not create the world or guide it. There are no essences, forms, or principles of reason to govern the universe.

In Books V and VI of *De Rerum Natura*, Lucretius offers us a poetic natural history whose goal is not to represent nature with propositions from outside but to continue nature's movement of spreading out and unfolding itself by other, poetic, means. In other words, if the practice of writing history is itself inside history, then writing history also creates history. Lucretius takes this idea seriously.

This is the meaning of Lucretius' performative contradiction of insist-ing that no mortal can write the objective history of nature. Yet Lucretius 'must speak as the majesty of things now known to us demands' (5.7–8). He does not represent the history of nature, but as part of nature, he 'unfolds' [*pandere*] (5.54) its 'folds' [*naturam triplicem*] (5.93) and is 'carried away by its woven order' [*detulit ordo*] (5.64). A materialist theory of history cannot be strictly linear because the past folds up inside the present. In this sense, the historian is not separate from the past. The past is part of the present, and the historian unfolds the immanent material conditions that they *are*. Materialist history must, therefore, be creative, not merely interpretive.

So then why do history? The purpose of history is not to glorify the struggle of life against death or each against all. Lucretius has no interest in the idealist history of labouring heroes like Hercules slaying monsters in faraway lands: the Nemean lion, the Arcadian boar, the bull of Crete, and the hydra of Lerna (5.21–7). Hercules was the hero of the Cynics, Stoics, Socrates, and Plato because his self-discipline through hard labour was a model of philosophy, ethics, and nature in general. Socrates preached the heroic military virtue of self-control. The Platonic hero, like Hercules, can endure intense heat, cold, and other physical privations.[7] The more the idealist virtue of self-discipline mortifies the body, the more it shows the immaterial mind and soul's superiority against and beyond nature.

In this idealist vision of history, life is hard, the body is weak-willed, nature is dangerous, and the correct orientation to the world should be one of domination aimed at immortality. In his *Memorabilia*, Xenophon (430–354 BCE), a student of Socrates, recounts the time that Socrates told his students about 'The Choice of Hercules'.[8] In the story, Hercules comes to a crossroads in his life and must decide if he will pursue a life of struggle and hard labour, or comfortable living, happiness, and pleasure. Unsurprisingly, Socrates approves of Hercules' choice to seek glory and 'immortal reputation' through battle.

However, Lucretius rejects the whole premise of this idealist version of history in which humans are separate from nature and can only escape by dominating it. Materialist history is not the story of individuals struggling against one another for glory and immortality. In Socrates' account, the path of 'happiness' is the path of 'pleasure', and is characterised negatively as the opposite of virtuous struggle: sloth. However, Lucretius explicitly rejects this false dichotomy and emphasises how much suffering and vice saturate the heroic, Herculean, Socratic worldview (5.45–8).

> *quantae tum scindunt hominem cuppedinis acres*
> *sollicitum curae quantique perinde timores!*
> *quidve superbia spurcitia ac petulantia? quantas*
> *efficiunt clades ! quid luxus desidiaeque?*

Figure 1.2 Statue of Hercules (Lansdowne Herakles), Roman Empire, about 125 CE, marble. Wikimedia Commons.

Figure 1.3 Annibale Carracci, *The Choice of Heracles* (1596). Wikimedia Commons.

> How many sharp cares of desire carve up
> a human being in distress, and equally how many fears?
> Or what of pride, filthy avarice, and arrogance? How many
> broken pieces do they bring about? What of soft living and idleness?

For Lucretius, historical materialism shows how human bodies and minds are iterations or folds in the broader material universe. There is no immortality, divine judgement, or escape from death and the body. There is no reason to fear what happens after death. We have nothing to gain after we die by self-mortification, struggle, and domination.

Furthermore, by treating life as a struggle, we 'divide' ourselves against ourselves, others, and nature. If we treat desire as a form of 'lack' [*cuppedinis*] (5.45) and seek reward in unattainable virtues, we will continuously be 'disturbed' by anxiety and fear (5.46). Our cares will become so sharp that they will cut us and the world into pieces [*clades*] (5.48).

Idealist histories with their heroics, struggles, dominations, and progress narratives promote pride, greed, and hubris. They are the result of a deep hatred of matter and motion and a fear of death.[9] No matter how many monsters we kill, it will not remove our fear of nature or death. If we define desire as a lack, no reward will ever be enough to fill our 'twisted' [*insinuandum*] (5.44) hearts. Epicurus, our materialist anti-hero, was the first to 'pull up' [*subegerit*] (5.49) and 'drive out' [*expulerit*] (5.50) of his mind this fear and hatred, not with weapons, but with *words*. Lucretius, therefore, summons words against war, and movement against discontinuity.

Here we have two models of history. There is the conquest model with Hercules as the hero, idealism as its philosophy, militarism as its ethics, and progress as its narrative. On the other hand, we have a naturalist model with Epicurus as its anti-hero, materialism as its philosophy, pleasure as its ethics, and entropic dissipation as its narrative.

Lucretius proposes to 'show with his words' [*doceo dictis*] this second kind of history. At the heart of Lucretius' historical materialism, he sets out two fundamental and unique laws [*leges*]. The first is that 'all things are bound to act [*foedere*] according to how they were made [*creata*]' (5.56–8). Lucretius explained in detail in Book II that all things come into being through the folding of indeterminately swerving matter.[10] This process is neither random nor deterministic but relationally pedetic. One process follows another but not in any predetermined way. This is why he says there is no *fati foedere*, 'bond of fate', or mechanical determinism in matter's motion. Instead, the *creata foedere* is a 'bond of creativity'. It is a strange 'law of indeterminism' in which all of nature is 'bound to be' an indeterminate *process* and cannot become a mechanical substance; otherwise, as Lucretius says in Book II, if it did, all would fall isolated in the empty void (2.222).

The second law of Lucretius' historical materialism is that nothing can escape the passage of time [*aevi*]. Nothing is static or unchangeable. More precisely, the passage of time is nothing other than the tendency of matter to spread out over time. Time and space, for Lucretius, are products of indeterminate moving matter. Matter does not move in time and space, but space and time emerge from swerving matter.

The second law of historical materialism is that everything in the universe tends towards entropy, dissipation, and destruction. Everything comes into being and passes away. Even 'the world consists of a mortal body', that 'come[s] into being . . . [and] will be destroyed' (5.65–97). Only matter, Lucretius says, is conserved, neither created (out of nothing) nor destroyed (into nothing) (1.150–243). So, in brief, the two laws of history are that everything emerges from indeterminate processes, and that matter is neither created nor destroyed but spreads out. Lucretius thus proposes an '*indeterminate thermodynamics*' of history.

Notes

1 See T. H. M. Gellar-Goad, *Laughing Atoms, Laughing Matter: Lucretius' De Rerum Natura and Satire* (Ann Arbor: University of Michigan Press, 2020).

2 See Thomas Nail, *Lucretius II: An Ethics of Motion* (Edinburgh: Edinburgh University Press, 2020), ch. 7.

3 See Thomas Nail, *Lucretius I: An Ontology of Motion* (Edinburgh: Edinburgh University Press, 2018), 233–41.

4 Georges Bataille, *Visions of Excess: Selected Writings, 1927–1939*, ed. Allan Stoekl, trans. Allan Stoekl, Carl R. Lovitt, and Donald M. Leslie Jr. (Minneapolis: University of Minnesota Press, 1985).

5 See Nail, *Lucretius I* and *Lucretius II*.

6 I thank one of my reviewers for this subtle and clever suggestion.

7 Robert Eisner, 'Socrates as Hero', *Philosophy and Literature*, 6.1–2 (1982): 109.

8 Xenophon, *Memorabilia* (Cambridge, MA: Harvard University Press, 1923), Book 4, Section 5, ll. 1–11.

9 See Nail, *Lucretius II*.

10 See Nail, *Lucretius I*.

2. The Birth of the World

What is the nature of the world? How did it begin, and how will it end? This is how Lucretius begins his materialist history at the start of Book V. Nature is a constant *flow* of matter [*fluere omnia constat*] (5.280) that tends to spread out over time. As matter flows, it swerves, folds, and creates metastable *cycles* along the way. Therefore, the history of the world has two fundamental motions: flows and cycles, dissipations and iterations. 'Matters' [*corpora*] flow and 'things' [*rerum*] cycle.

Every *thing* in our universe emerged at some point and will pass away. The cycle of creation and destruction is at the material heart of many mythopoetic traditions. For Lucretius, everything begins in the middle. Matter was not created and will not dissolve. History, however, is born and will die. Matter flows and history cycles. Together they form a spiral meander, presciently depicted by the Minoans. Each spiral opens to and is opened by another. Creation and destruction proceed through one another, unravelling towards their ultimate dissipation.

History, for Lucretius, is a history of *motion*. History is the shape of kinetic patterns traced out by the universe as it experiments with new ways to spread itself out, like a pat of butter melting into fatty dendrites over the surface of a warm pan. History is the flowing, folding, and weaving of matter into various patterns, rhythms, and textures. As such, it is not reducible to human history. Human history is only one set of emergent patterns in a much deeper cosmic movement towards the complete dissipation of the universe. The act of telling stories about the meaning and emergence of the world and human culture is a kinetic act that helps the universe spread out and dissipate its heat.

This chapter aims to describe and expand Lucretius' claims about the central role of motion in natural history through a close reading of lines 91–508 of Book V. The chapter puts forward the core features of a new theory of historical new materialism against the human-centric, idealist,

Figure 2.1 Spiral, rosette and double-axe motifs on *pithoi*. From upper left to middle left: three Knossian 'palace style' *pithoi* (Late Minoan II). Middle right: *pithos* from Knossos (Late Minoan IA). Lower left: *pithos* from Pseira (Late Minoan IA). Lower right: 'palace style' *pithos* (Late Minoan II) from Knossos. After A. Evans, *The Palace of Minos* (London: Macmillan, 1921), IV:1, fig. 282; III, fig. 199; IV:1, fig. 260; II:2, figs. 245, 284; IV:1, fig. 285.

metaphysical, and mechanistic versions often espoused in the Western tradition.[1] In short, I would like to introduce the reader to Lucretius' startlingly contemporary and novel theory of history.

The Woven Way of the World

The first and perhaps most significant feature to point out in Lucretius' theory of history is that it is *'woven'*. What does this mean? It means that a blueprint or intelligent design of some higher being does not determine history. It also means that mechanical laws of nature do not define it. All laws of nature emerged historically.[2] There is, to put it more dramatically, no such thing as 'nature' or 'the world' as a complete set of things in the universe because nature is not a thing but a *process*.

This is a genuinely astonishing claim: 'The world does not exist, but history does.' Lucretius entirely subordinates nature to the historical process. There is no bit of nature unmoved or untouched by history, movement, and change. There are only processes iterated into metastable patterns that look like stable 'laws', 'causality', and 'objects'. In truth, there is only history in motion. This means that the world is not an object or set of objects, but an emergent pattern born from a cosmic weaving (5.91–6).

> *Quod superest, ne te in promissis plura moremur,*
> *principio maria ac terras caelumque tuere:*
> *quorum naturam triplicem, tria corpora, Memmi,*
> *tris species tam dissimilis, tria talia texta,*
> *una dies dabit exitio, multosque per annos*
> *sustentata ruet moles et machina mundi.*

> For what remains, so that I not delay you any longer with promises,
> begin by taking a look at the seas and lands and sky.
> Their threefold nature, their three bodies, Memmius, their three
> aspects so different, three such weavings,
> a single day will give over to destruction, and the massive structure
> of the world, sustained through many years, will come crashing down.

Water, land, and sky appear as distinct figures to us, yet they are but 'folds' [*triplicem*] (5.93) 'woven' [*texta*] (5.94) from the 'first-threads' [*primordia*] of matter, Lucretius says. Each Empedoclean element has a different 'aspect or figure' [*species*] (5.94) drawn from a broader process that is carrying them towards their destruction.

This is a striking way to start the birth of world history. We do not live in a world of discrete forms or objects but of interwoven aspects or figures folded up within one another. In just the first few lines of his history, Lucretius gives us the two laws of historical new materialism. Nature spreads out and hands the world over to destruction. It does this by experimentally folding and weaving each aspect into the others. It may sound counter-intuitive, but water, earth, and sky help unfold the universe faster than if it had merely tried to spread out evenly.[3] Just as water in a basin drains more easily through a spiralling vortex than it does without one, the world spreads itself out faster by iteratively unfolding through elemental turbulence.

Sea, earth, and sky are each made and remade *through one another*. Each is a different texture in the woven pattern of water cycle, rock cycle, and atmospheric cycle. Each of these cycles helps dissipate the others. Each 'weaves' [*texta*] and 'unweaves' [*retextum*] the other. This is why Lucretius describes them as a 'woven threefold' [*texta triplicem*] (5.93–4).

Furthermore, the threefold entanglement of earth, sky, and sea follows a similar threefold complication of the flow, fold, and collision of matter more broadly. The earth flows across the surface, the moon folds and cycles through the sky, as the sky and earth touch at sea. According to Hesiod's *Theogony*, Gaia emerges from indeterminate Chaos. From Chaos comes Gaia, and from Gaia comes Ouranos (Sky) and Pontus (Sea). Each unfolds from the other. In archaic cosmology, then, earth, sky, and sea are a threefold woven from the indeterminate flows of formless Chaos.

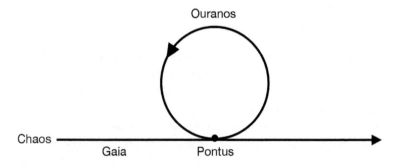

Figure 2.2 Chaos gives birth to the flow of Earth that births the Sky and the Sea. This geological drama describes the shoreline where earth meets the sea under the sky.

It is highly significant that Hesiod places the process of indeterminate Chaos at the beginning of his cosmology. If Chaos is first, then nothing that comes after can be genuinely static or fully self-identical. Everything else that becomes is related to process, change, and movement because Chaos creates the immanent instability within which all other gods *become*. Thus, the Greek word *khaos* takes on later historical definitions as void, emptiness, chasm, space, and formless matter.[4] *Khaos* is perhaps one of the earliest Greek words that will later tie together the ideas of matter and motion against the logic of being and identity. Chaos is formless, being-less, empty, and yet creative. It is in motion and woven deeply into all of nature. Chaos is a creative indeterminate void. It has no form but is the immanent process within and by which forms come to be, metamorphose, and dissolve.

The primacy of Chaos has enormous consequences for archaic cosmology. It means that, at least for Hesiod and his tradition, there is no single, stable substance beneath the world of change and metamorphosis. It means that nature is an open-ended process of indeterminate mixture and hybridity. Chaos is the *primordial indeterminacy* from which the world is organised and differentiated into various regions. Chaos is the process of mixing.

The swerve is Lucretius' indeterminate primordial chaos. It is a rejection of all cosmologies that begin with eternal and static forms or gods. For Lucretius, there is no starting principle of the universe. Everything emerges through the indeterminate *process of history*. Instead of thinking of history as being directed towards accumulation, development, and progress, Lucretius completely flips the script. World history is the history of dissipation and experimentation in the face of continual degradation. Everything is excess. The world is dying, and the earth (sea, land, and sky) is here to help hasten it. We are all here to creatively advance the unweaving of the world by folding it again and again.

Return to the Delphic Oracle

The birth of a dying world is 'a strange thing to contemplate', Lucretius says (5.97–8). The process occurs over such a long time that it feels 'unworldly' to imagine. And yet, if we consult our senses carefully, we will see that everything around us follows the same tendency towards dissipation, as water evaporates from our wet clothes in the sun.

Demonstrating that the world will die is something 'difficult . . . to prove conclusively with words', Lucretius says, and yet he must 'speak out' (5.98–104). Eventually, when we feel the earth shake beneath our feet, we will be made viscerally aware of the 'massive movements of the earth' (5.106) and its tendency towards destruction. The earth's movement means that even the most solid foundation is mobile and subject to change and decay. The poet pays close attention to this process hidden in plain sight. For the third time in *De Rerum Natura* Lucretius connects his poetry to the oracle of Delphi (1.920–34; 4.1–4; 5.110–16).

Qua prius adgrediar quam de re fundere fata
sanctius et multo certa ratione magis quam
Pythia quae tripode a Phoebi lauroque profatur,
multa tibi expediam doctis solacia dictis,
religione refrenatus ne forte rearis
terras et solem et caelum, mare sidera lunam,
corpore divino debere aeterna manere,

Before I proceed to pour out sacred oracles about this thing
and in a much more certain manner than
the Pythia who speaks out from the tripod and laurel of Apollo,
I will unfold many solaces to you with learned words,
lest held in check and bridled by religion you by chance suppose
that the earth and sun and sky, sea, stars, and moon,
must abide in place forever, endowed with divine body,

What is the connection between historical materialism and oracular truth? These are undoubtedly strange bedfellows. Yet Lucretius wants to bring them together in a way that transforms them. It is easy to read Lucretius as if he were criticising oracular practice in favour of the 'rational' discourse of the philosophers. Yet Lucretius' explicit criticism of philosophical reason at 1.734–41 and his own claim to be 'pouring out sacred oracles' [*fundere fata sanctius*] (5.110–11) complicates such a simple interpretation. Furthermore, we should recall that Lucretius likens his poetic-theoretical method to being stabbed through the heart by Dionysus' intoxicating *thyrsus*. This causes his 'mind to bloom' with knowledge of the nature of things (1.920–34).

What is going on then? Lucretius is relating his performative speech-acts about the nature of things to the Delphic oracle. What do his poem, nature, and the Delphic oracle have in common? Lucretius 'pours out'

Figure 2.3 Dancing maenad, after a white-ground tondo from an Attic red-figure kylix. Wikimedia Commons.

[*fundere*] (5.110) and 'unfolds' [*expediam*] (5.113) his 'sacred speech' [*fata sanctius*] (5.111) into the air just as nature flows and folds into things [*rerum*] and just as the rotting body of the dragoness Python flows out of Gaia and folds into turbulent fumes. The fumes and bitter laurels are then inhaled by priestesses, which allows them to speak the earth's wisdom.[5] The earth (Gaia) speaks a material truth through the dissipation of volcanic fumes and plant intoxicants. The Delphic priestesses were called 'bees' because of their connection to poetic-prophetic speech, and to Dionysus, whose rituals involved bees, honey, mead, and oracle. Lucretius, too, calls himself a bee (3.11). Poetry, nature, and the oracle are all performative and kinetic kinds of knowledge. They are not representations but rather materialisations.

Lucretius embraces the prophetic tradition for its emphasis on the material, embedded, and performative nature of speech and knowledge.

Figure 2.4 Aegeus (right) consults the Pythia or oracle of Delphi, red-figure kylix, 440–430 BCE. Wikimedia Commons.

Knowledge comes from natural patterns and sensuous states of inspiration and ecstasy, not from abstract thought. However, he also embraces the poetic and philosophical tradition's emphasis on well-woven speech-acts that are 'more certain' and clear than the theoleptic trances of the priestesses. For Lucretius, reason does not oppose the senses. Reason is a kind of sensation, a blooming of the senses, that entangles the other senses (3.94–221).[6] He says that the senses are paths that lead to the 'serene oracular temple of the mind' [*sapientum templa serena; templaque mentis*] (2.8; 3.103) and the soul is a material movement in the body akin to the sweet smell of Bacchus' flowers (3.221).[7] For Lucretius, the soul is Dionysian because its death is creative, like Python and Gaia, Demeter and Persephone.

Figure 2.5 John Collier, *The Priestess at Delphi* (1891), showing the Pythia sitting on a tripod with vapour rising from a crack in the earth beneath her. Wikimedia Commons.

Here is the takeaway. Lucretius compares himself to the oracle at Delphi to emphasise the performative nature of his methodology. He is not representing nature but doing what nature is doing: weaving. He grounds his observation of the world's dissipation in the visible volcanic dissolution and evaporation of the earth at Delphi. The oracle of Delphi was inside a mountain where volcanic fumes and fresh springs came up from the earth. Python spoke the words of Gaia through the dissipation of the earth into turbulent eddies of smoke. The priestess on her tripod sat above the fumes and inhaled the world's dying breath.

The death of the earth may sound depressing, but for Lucretius, it is liberating. If the world is dying, there is no divine judgement after the end of everything. There are no unchanging forms to imprison thought and reality. Humans are not cut off from the rest of nature but are rather an expressive and creative part of it. This is why Lucretius says his words are a soothing solace [*solacia*] (5.113). His words free thought and action from the 'bridled' [*refrenatus*] (5.114) and bound '*ligare*' [*religione*] (5.114) structure of unchanging forms and the hatred of the body and matter. If all of nature is dissipating and dying, then there is no fixed hierarchy of being or knowledge. The movement of history is freedom from fear, judgement, and dogmatism.

Gigantomachy; or, Why 'I Hate the Pack of Gods'

The world is a process of dissipation, and there is no punishment after death for being a materialist atheist. In this way, Lucretius reclaims the 'earth-born' *Gigantes* of Greek mythology for his materialism, against Hercules and the Olympians, who tried to punish the Giants (5.117–21).

> *proptereaque putes ritu par esse Gigantum*
> *pendere eos poenas inmani pro scelere omnis*
> *qui ratione sua disturbent moenia mundi*
> *praeciarumque velint caeli restinguere solem,*
> *inmortalia mortali sermone notantes;*

and therefore think it is right, just as in the case of the Giants,
that all those should pay the penalty for their monstrous crime
who by rising up to disturb the walls of the world
and who wish to extinguish the brilliant sun shining in the sky,
shamefully branding immortal things with mortal speech.

The Gigantomachy is not the same as the Titanomachy, although the two are often confused. In his *Theogony*, Hesiod says the Giants were born from 'all the bloody drops that gushed forth' when Cronos castrated his father, Ouranos. Gaia 'received' the drops of blood as they hit the ground. As 'the seasons moved round', Gaia bore the Giants (*Theogony*, 185). Venus was born from the falling semen and carried by Gaia as well. Together, Venus and the Giants were born from the hatred and castration of the god.

In their ways, Aphrodite and the Giants threaten to undermine the hierarchy of the gods. As the 'desire of men and gods' (1.1), the love of Venus introduced radical immanence into the world that traversed and suffused all of nature.[8] As 'monsters', the Giants' strife also introduces radical immanence because it turned nature against itself in battle. The love of Venus and the strife of the Giants form an Empedoclean spiral. The nature of the earth (Gaia) is, therefore, to continually create and destroy. This is the strange way Lucretius turns mythology and the gods against themselves in what we might call his '*mythological naturalism*'.

The Giants, according to Lucretius, wanted to rise up [*ratione sua*] and destroy the gods just as Epicurus once rose up against the walls of the world [*moenia mundi*] (1.73). They wanted to create turbulence [*disturbent*] in the walls of the world by 'branding immortal things with mortal speech'. This is also what Lucretius says Epicurus did against the gods (1.73–4). The Giants, like the swerving of matter and the fall of blood from the sky, use turbulence against authority. When the gods impose their skyward authority to limit nature's movement against monstrosity, the monsters rise up.

In Lucretius' description, the Giants are chthonic border crossers, criminals, mutants, who use their words as weapons against divine power and Herculean/Socratic military virtue. The Giants were depicted in ancient art with snakes for legs and were associated with volcanic and seismic activity. In particular, the Giants lived under Mt Etna, where Empedocles also lived and located strife.[9]

As serpent monsters under the earth and enemies of the gods, the Giants are similar to other chthonic serpents such as Typhon, Echidna, and Python at the Delphic oracle. The serpent body is a coiling, writhing, spiral body whose unpredictable swerving undermines the earth from within and below. Just as the Giants live underground and destroy the earth through volcanism and earthquakes, so does Python. This

Figure 2.6 In the Gigantomachy from a first-century CE frieze in the agora of Aphrodisias, the Giants are depicted with scaly coils, like Typhon. Wikimedia Commons.

turbulence also fits Lucretius' argument that earthquakes are direct sensuous evidence that the earth's foundations are in motion, unstable, and
will eventually destroy the world. This is the world for Lucretius. It is a
place that actively undermines its foundations through movement and
that will ultimately dissipate because matter swerves. For Lucretius, the
world is, therefore, 'anti-foundational' precisely because it is a material-
kinetic *process.*

Theology of the Simulacrum

World history is a process of dissipation and iteration. Nothing on earth
or in the heavens is static, unchanging, or divine, but all is in flux. This is
Lucretius' thesis. He offers evidence for all this shortly. However, before
he does, he pauses to explicitly denounce the idea that the gods exist
anywhere in the world (5.146–9).

> *Illud item non est ut possis credere, sedes*
> *esse deum sanctas in mundi partibus ullis,*
> *tenvis enim natura deum longeque remota*
> *sensibus ab nostris animi vix mente videtur;*

> This likewise is not possible for you to believe:
> that the holy dwellings of the gods are in any part of our world.
> For the nature of the gods, weak and far removed from our senses,
> is seen with great difficulty by the faculty of the mind.

Lucretius invokes the gods throughout *De Rerum Natura*, but not until
Book V does he describe the precise *mode* of their existence. *Religio*, as
a practice, is distinct from the life of the gods. *Religio* is a real social
institution of physical and mental bondage. It is not merely a subjective
delusion but a real material mutilation of nature.[10] Now, on the mode of
the existence of the gods, Lucretius is clear and consistent that they do
not exist in the world, but rather we see simulacra images of them in our
imagination and dreams (5.146–55; 5.1169–82; 6.76–7).

Simulacra are real material processes internal and external to us
whose diffractions and combinations can produce new images that we
have never seen or touched before, such as ghosts and giants' faces in
the clouds (4.1–200).[11] The simulacra of the imagination, according to
Lucretius, are 'thin and weak' [*tenvis*] (4.85; 5.148) like the mind (4.748).
'Simulacra from their sanctified bodies' [*de corpore . . . sancto simulacra*]

(6.76) are just that, images performatively rendered sacred by humans. They do not affect or get affected by the rest of the world *to the same degree* as other, more robust, images.

They are, however, still material and real, but only in the sense that the operation of our minds and souls is also material, although thin and weak. We can think of the electrochemical and neurological activity that coordinates our bodily movements but that cannot *directly* do much in the world. The total electrical energy of our body is equivalent to a 100 watt light bulb. So too, the *sancto simulacra* have a minimal direct effect on the world.

In short, for Lucretius, the gods do not exist in the world of nature as fully autonomous deities or beyond the world as transcendent persons. They do not even live 'in-between' worlds, as Epicurus said. Lucretius never uses the Latin word *intermundia*, meaning 'between worlds'. That term, along with the terms *atomus* (atom) and *indiuiduum* (particle), is Cicero's creation, not Lucretius'. Lucretius is also explicit that we should never participate in any religious rituals, even to contemplate the gods' perfection, as Epicurus and his followers did.[12]

'Nature appears, liberated at once and freed from haughty masters, to do everything herself by herself on her own without the gods' (2.1090). Nature does not need gods. History, too, is liberated from the gods because it dissolves them. Nothing in nature resists dissipation. In three clear passages, Lucretius says that the gods' mode of existence is as weak or tenuous images. They are the material simulacra in our imaginations. The images of gods come into existence at a certain point in history with human dreams and imagination, and will die out with us (5.1169–82).

Since our souls and minds are material, then so are the *sancto simulacra* as material ideas. Insofar as these ideas spread and have cultural effects or result in religious institutions, they have real, although indirect, material consequences on the world. Their 'dwelling places ought to be different from our dwelling places, being weak [*tenues*] in accord with their bodies' (5.154). Their dwelling place perfectly fits their simulacra bodies, which are thin electrical patterns in our brain.

Just like the monstrous, mutant, and swerving snake-legged Giants, Lucretius aims to use his 'words to shake' [*verbis vexare*] the pernicious idea of divine creation so that it is 'overturned from top to bottom' [*et ab imo evertere summa*] (5.163). Materiality shall rise from its chthonic and Pythonic depths like a turbulent vapour to shake divine power.

Process Materialism and Metastable History

Even if there were creator gods, Lucretius argues, they would have no model for their creation unless the material patterns of nature had already existed. This is a startling inversion of Plato's cosmology in the *Timaeus*. There, Plato describes a universe created by a 'divine crafts-man' [*demiurge*]. The craftsman looks to a perfect static model [*eidos*] and uses a defective material [*chora*] to create a copy. This copy is our moving cosmos.

However, Lucretius completely rejects the idea of a static model and provides an alternative history where there is only moving matter. Forms are emergent patterns in nature, not unchanging essences. For Lucretius, all creation in nature assumes an intense *historical* process of emergent patterns [*speciem*]. The source of these emergent patterns is the habitual and indeterminate swerving of matter. Nature moves by 'thoroughly changing itself and its distribution' [*permutato ordine*] to 'create new patterns and forms of being' [*specimen natura creandi*] (5.185–6). Lucretius thus flips Platonism, idealism, and divine creation on their heads by suggesting that *matter is creative*. Even if there were gods, their intelligence would derive entirely from nature's movement, mutation, and original patterns.

History is thoroughly material and experimental. There is no divine plan or set of pre-existing natural laws to guide the movement of the universe. Without determinism or causality, history becomes relational and indeterminate. The swerve reigns supreme. Nature tends to dissipate and iterate, flow and fold, but it does not know in advance what the optimal way to do this is. It has to experiment with itself. This is history for Lucretius (5.187–94).

> namque ita multa modis multis primordia rerum
> ex infinito iam tempore percita plagis
> ponderibusque suis consuerunt concita ferri
> omnimodisque coire atque omnia pertemptare,
> quaecumque inter se possent congressa creare,
> ut non sit mirum si in talis disposituras
> deciderunt quoque et in talis venere meatus,
> qualibus haec rerum geritur nunc summa novando.

For so many first weavings of things in so many
rhythms, propelled by blows from boundless time until the present day

and impelled by their own weight, have been accustomed to being borne
    along,
and to sew together in all sorts of ways and to feel out all combinations,
whatever they are able to create when brought together among themselves,
that it is no wonder if they also fell into such arrangements
and settled into such movements, as these now by which
the sum of things bears by renewing itself.

History weaves together in so many ways, rhythms, and patterns
because matter is '*habitually swerving*' [*declinare solerent*] (2.221). Matter is
continually shape-changing and becoming other as it flows along [*permutato ordine . . . specimen natura creandi . . . concita ferri*] (5.185–9). History is,
therefore, genuinely creative and relational because matter is 'actively
colliding' [*percita plagis*] with itself (5.188) and sewing [*consuerunt*] itself
into new moving patterns [*congressa creare*] all the time.

Material processes have no beginning and no end [*ex infinito iam tempore*]
(5.188). They are neither created nor destroyed. However, history is the
process by which the world of things [*rerum*] emerges, combines, and dissipates. Matter flows along [*concita ferri*] and folds or sews up [*consuerunt*]
into things through 'experimentation' [*pertemptare*]. It 'tries out or feels
the pulse of' the rhythms of the 'active collisions', without knowing or
controlling them in advance.

The weaving imagery in this passage is striking. The first threads
experimentally sew themselves together into various moving patterns,
which then iteratively 'support, bear, or wear' further patterns in an
ongoing renewal. Nature is a cosmic weaver that wears or supports
history like a shape-changing garment. History weaves and unweaves.
It is destroyed and renewed like the death shroud that Penelope weaves
during the day and unweaves at night in the *Odyssey*.

The Lady of the Labyrinth

Look around, Lucretius says, the world was not made *for us*. There is no
evidence whatsoever for divine creation or the centrality of the human
perspective. Even if we did not know about the first threads [*primordia*]
(5.195), we could easily use our senses to see how much turbulence there
is in nature.

The earth is not a static stage for human drama. Nothing stands
still but instead has unpredictable and often destructive movements.

Everything our senses know suggests that nature loves to swerve [*declinare solerant*]. We should not be shocked that the earth flows all over the place without regard to our preferences (5.195–234).

The sky has 'rapid and unpredictable motions' [*impetus*] (5.200), and the mountains, forests, ocean, and animals 'desirously' [*avidam*] occupy the majority of the earth (5.201). To be precise, humans are only .01 per cent of the total biomass on earth. It should be clear, looking around, that humans are latecomers to the planet and are only a tiny portion of it. Some areas are too cold, and others are too hot because severe frosts are 'carried away by swift movements' [*aufert*] (5.205). Wild plants 'wrap around and swallow up' [*obducat*] (5.207) everything unless humans actively resist them.

Even when humans try to grow plants, their crops are often destroyed by 'rapid boiling movements of heat' [*torret fervoribus*] (5.215), or else they are 'blasted by turbulent whirling winds' [*flabraque ventorum violento turbine vexant*] (5.217). Dangerous animals 'violently disturb our safety' [*infestum*] (5.219), and illness is carried along [*adportant*] (5.221) by the seasons without warning. So much of nature's movements is unpredictable. Even death is like a vagabond wanderer, roaming and fluctuating here and there [*vagatur*] (5.221), striking without warning.

Every other baby animal seems better prepared to live on earth than human babies. Humans have had the least time to adapt to the earth, so their children 'pour and flow forth out' [*profudit*] (5.225) of their mother's wombs 'onto the shores of light' without even the ability to walk. They are immediately 'thrown like sailors on turbulent waves' [*saevis proiectus ab undis navita*] (5.222) and begin to wail. All Lucretius' evidence for how nature is not *for* humans draws on fluid dynamic images related to the turbulent swerving and folding of matter.

This is also why Lucretius describes nature as *daedala* (1.7; 1.228; 5.233–4).

. . . *quando omnibus omnia large*
tellus ipsa parit naturaque daedala rerum.

. . . the earth herself and nature
the artificer of things provides everything in abundance for all.

The Latin word *daedala* means 'skilful maker' and comes from the Greek name Daídalos, the mythic creator of the Minoan labyrinth on Crete. Daídalos was based on the original creator of the labyrinth, or Potnia, as

Figure 2.7 Silver drachma, Knossos, 300–270 BCE. Obverse: head of Hera, wearing ornamented stephanos, triple-pendant earring, and necklace. Reverse: labyrinth, flanked by A–P, ΚΝΩΣΙ(ΩΝ), 'of Knossians', below. Wikimedia Commons.

the Minoans called her. She was known as 'the lady of the labyrinth'.[13] She conducted one of the most important ceremonies in Minoan Crete: the labyrinth ritual. The labyrinth may have been the name of a place near Knossos where there was a sanctuary, a cave, or an open-air cult site dedicated to Potnia.[14] It may also have been, according to Homer, a painted design on the ground where a ritual dance occurred. Young men and women performed the ritual by entering the folded labyrinth, spiralling towards one another, and then away in the epiphany of creation and destruction. Labyrinth and meander images appear on an early seal from the Minoan palace of Haghia Triada, on a Mycenaean clay tablet from Pylos in the Peloponnese, and on a painted plaster wall from the Minoan Palace of Phaistos;[15] still others appear on late coins from Knossos dating from the Classical Greek period around 350 BCE.[16]

The Minoan labyrinth ritual was a performance of the immanent processes of the flowing, folding, and weaving of nature. Instead of *thinking* about the world as a changing substance or as a chaotic flux, the Minoans *performed* the world's folding and unfolding movement in the differential iteration of the braided labyrinth. The path of the labyrinth moves inwards, folding over itself, and then outwards again.

Homer fills his description of the Minoan labyrinth dance in the *Iliad* with images of weaving. He says that Hephaestus weaves [*daidala poiei*] and folds [*triplaka . . . ptukhes*] liquid flows of metal together to make Achilles' shield just as Daedalus wove the labyrinth dance floor of Knossos for the Minoan goddess of weaving, Ariadne. The name Ariadne was likely a later name for Potnia of the labyrinth.[17]

What is the meaning of the Minoan labyrinth and Lucretius' reference to nature as *daedala*? It is a philosophical, epistemological, and aesthetic performance of nature as a process of folding, unfolding, and weaving. The labyrinth was not a place to worship transcendent forms, fixed substances, or chaotic flux. It was an enacted knowledge of immanent processes. It is the incarnation of an understanding that nature is not for us alone. We are its threads. The labyrinth was not a maze but a spiral meander pattern that one's life follows. It was a performance of nature's turbulence and the human place in the cycle of creation and destruction.

As the dancers moved towards the centre of the labyrinth, they folded up in its tangled lines like the roots and branches of archaic Crete's sacred groves. As the dancers enter the centre, they 'go to sleep' or 'die' in Potnia's fertile soil. The flows of life slow, curl up, and become dormant in the ground. Death is the enfolding of matter into darkened earth-graves. All life comes from the earth and eventually enfolds back into the soil. The Minoans planted their dead in the folded foetal position like seeds in the soil, inside beehive tombs. Just as bees hibernate in winter and emerge in spring, 'the lady of the labyrinth', who received 'a jar of honey', guided the burial practice and gestured towards metamorphosis after death.

As the dancers or ritual performers moved outwards from the centre of the labyrinth, they unfolded like seed sprouts. From the seed pod and the beehive, interred over the winter, come the plant, flower, and bee in the spring.[18] The two blades of the famous double-bladed axe held by the 'lady of the labyrinth' are the two folds of the continual process of life and death, spring and autumn, light and dark. The double axe is a 'visual palindrome',[19] showing the flow of life into death and death into life.

With the phrase '*naturaque daedala*' Lucretius invokes the meandering process of nature that brings creation and destruction regardless of human struggle and without divine creation. Nature *daedala* creates everything in abundance. Destruction is only a reallocation. Lucretius completely overturns the idea of nature as lack and instead embraces an ontology of excess and generosity. The notion that nature is scarce is a limited, human-centric perspective. Relative to human desires, certain things seem rare or lacking. However, relative to nature, there is no lack and no scarcity. Lack in one region is surplus in another. Certain humans think nature is a competitive war against all because they view nature as being for them. The lady of the labyrinth teaches another lesson with her spiralling meander: that the cosmos is excess and generosity.

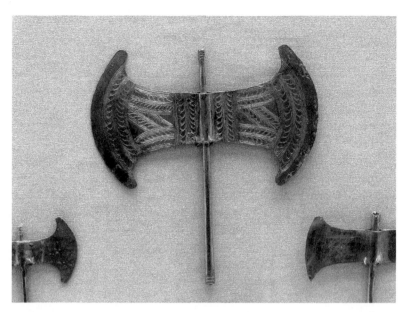

Figure 2.8 An ornamented golden Minoan double axe or labrys. Wikimedia Commons.

Conclusion

For Lucretius, history is the crystalline residue or footsteps left by the dissipation and iteration of matter. It is a woven and unwoven web stretched out across the universe like a cosmic labyrinth of mycelium. The *turbulence of material history* proves that the gods did not make nature for humans.

In this chapter, I have tried to describe the first few broad strokes of Lucretius' kinetic approach to history. In the next chapter, I look more closely at the precise material history of the universe and its journey towards death.

Notes

1 This theory contributes to a new materialist understanding of history. For a review and discussion of new materialism, see Christopher N. Gamble, Joshua S. Hanan, and Thomas Nail, 'What is New Materialism?', *Angelaki: Journal of the Theoretical Humanities*, 24.6 (2019): 111–34.

2 For a contemporary argument that the laws of nature have changed over time, see Roberto Mangabeira Unger and Lee Smolin, *The Singular Universe and the Reality of Time* (Cambridge: Cambridge University Press, 2015). They argue not only that cosmology is an irreducibly historical discipline, but that this principle should drive the research agenda.

3 See Thomas Nail, *Theory of the Earth* (Palo Alto, CA: Stanford University Press, forthcoming), ch. 14.

4 See Henry G. Liddell and Robert Scott, *Greek–English Lexicon, With a Revised Supplement* (Oxford: Clarendon Press, 1996).

5 The priestess of Pythia may have eaten and inhaled oleander. See Haralampos V. Harissis, 'A Bittersweet Story: The True Nature of the Laurel of the Oracle of Delphi', *Perspectives in Biology and Medicine*, 57.3 (2014): 351–60.

6 See also Thomas Nail, *Lucretius II: An Ethics of Motion* (Edinburgh: Edinburgh University Press, 2020), ch. 3 on the critique of kinetic reason.

7 Lucretius also shows his methodological affinity to the poetic-philosophical tradition by referencing Empedocles. '[H]ighway of belief to the temple of the mind' is taken from Empedocles. See also Monica R. Gale, *Myth and Poetry in Lucretius* (Cambridge: Cambridge University Press, 1994), 59–64, on Lucretius' relationship to Empedocles.

8 See Thomas Nail, *Lucretius I: An Ontology of Motion* (Edinburgh: Edinburgh University Press, 2018), ch. 1.

9 Nail, *Lucretius I*, 133.

10 See Karl Marx, 'Theses on Feuerbach', in *Marx and Engels Collected Works: Volume 5, Marx and Engels 1845–47 (MECW 5)* (London: Lawrence and Wishart, 1976), 3–8. Marx follows Lucretius against Feuerbach on the critique of religion.

11 See Nail, *Lucretius II*, ch. 6.

12 Epicurus encouraged his followers to participate in religious rituals in order to strengthen their mental conception of *ataraxia*. See Kirk Summers, 'Lucretius and the Epicurean Tradition of Piety', *Classical Philology*, 90.1 (1995): 32–57.

13 In classical Greece, the title *potnia* is usually applied to the goddesses Demeter, Artemis, Athena, Persephone, and Gaia. See 'πότνια', in Liddell and Scott, *A Greek–English Lexicon*. See also Bernard Dietrich, *The Origins of Greek Religion* (Bristol, RI: Bristol Phoenix Press, 2004), 181–5; George E. Mylonas, *Mycenae and the Mycenaean Age* (Princeton:

Princeton University Press, 1966), 159; and John Chadwick and Michael Ventris, *Documents in Mycenean Greek*, 2nd edn (Cambridge: Cambridge University Press, 1976).

14 See Barbara Montecchi, 'The Labyrinth: Building, Myth, and Symbol', in Eva Alram-Stern, Fritz Blakolmer, Sigrid Deger-Jalkotzy, Robert Laffineur, and Jörg Weilhartner (eds), *METAPHYSIS: Ritual, Myth and Symbolism in the Aegean Bronze Age. 15th International Aegean Conference, University of Vienna, 22–25 April 2014* (Leuven: Peeters, 2016), 165–74.

15 See images in Montecchi, 'The Labyrinth: Building, Myth, and Symbol'.

16 'On Crete in particular, we have several examples on seals and seal-ings from the EM II onward, in addition to the meanders depicted on a painted floor from the Palace of Phaistos, and on the fresco fragments from the Lower passage-way, just East of The Hall of the Double Axes, both dating to the MM III', Montecchi, 'The Labyrinth: Building, Myth, and Symbol', 170. See also J. L. Crowley, *The Iconography of Aegean Seals* (Leuven: Peeters, 2013), 124 I 123, 286 E 314; Pietro Militello, *Gli affreschi minoici di Festòs* (Padua: Bottega d'Erasmo, 2001), 148–9, pl. A.2; Arthur Evans, *The Palace at Minos: A Comparative Account of the Successive Stages of Early Cretan Civilization as Illustrated by the Discoveries at Knossos, Vol. 1: The Neolithic and Early and Middle Minoan Ages* (London: Macmillan, 1921), 356–7, fig. 256; and L. Morgan, 'Minoan Paintings and Egypt: the Case of Tell el-Daba', in W. Vivian Davies and Louise Schofield (eds), *Egypt, the Aegean and the Levant: Interconnections in the Second Millennium BC* (London: Trustees of the British Museum, 1995), 43–4.

17 See Carl Kerényi, *Dionysos: Archetypal Image of Indestructible Life*, trans. Ralph Manheim (Princeton: Princeton University Press, 1976).

18 'This is the "year god", who dies and is reborn every year, and whose rebirth was celebrated in the mountain caves and probably also in the labyrinth of the temple-palace at Knossos.' Anne Baring and Jules Cashford, *The Myth of the Goddess: Evolution of an Image* (London: Arkana, 2000), 135.

19 On the religious and symbolic meaning of the double axe, see Miton P. Nilsson, *The Minoan-Mycenaean Religion and its Survival in Greek Religion*, rev. 2nd edn (Lund: Gleerup, 1968), 194–235; Nanno Marinatos, *Minoan Religion: Ritual, Image, and Symbol* (Columbia, SC: University of South Carolina Press, 1993), 5, 49–50, 145, 235; Helène Whittaker, 'Horns and Axes', in Alram-Stern et al. (eds), *METAPHYSIS: Ritual,*

Myth and Symbolism in the Aegean Bronze Age, 109–14. See also Robert B. Koehl, 'The Ambiguity of the Minoan Mind', in Alram-Stern et al. (eds), *METAPHYSIS: Ritual, Myth and Symbolism in the Aegean Bronze Age*, 471.

3. The Death of the World

Two thousand years before we discovered that the universe was expanding, Lucretius gave us an amazing description of its dissipation. Before we discovered plate tectonics, Gaian systems theory, thermodynamics, and awareness of earth's earliest Epoch, Lucretius wrote a shockingly consistent description of a turbulent and perishable earth. Not only was his description ahead of its time, but it remains ahead of our time in several ways. Only in the last couple of decades have we realised just how truly fragile and turbulent earth's climate is. Climate change and recent geological transformations force us to conclude what Lucretius concluded long ago: *the world is not for us.*

Western history has acted as if the earth were a stable place for us to mould into whatever we want, just as Plato's demiurge moulded the passive matter of the cosmos into an abstract idea or model of eternal perfection. In all its forms, the history of idealism has tried to convince us that the world is ours and that we can manipulate it as we please without disturbing the stable order of things. Climate change is due mainly to a deep philosophical and cultural misunderstanding about the nature of things and how history works.

If we think matter is passive, mechanical, and ours to manipulate, we will treat the natural world accordingly. We will disturb the metastable balance of things. If we think that human life or even life in general is the purpose of the universe, we will try to conserve it against everything else, to our detriment. Unfortunately, we are living with the fallout from this enormous metaphysical error of thinking humans are separate from nature. Modern science and technology are, in no small degree, the instrumental handmaidens to colonialism, capitalism, and climate change.

However, the roots of an alternative philosophy and science have been with us the whole time. Lucretius' poem is an attempt to recover the roots of an archaic alternative. Lucretius is, I believe, part of the anti-dote to our present ecological crisis. Lucretius' mythological naturalism contributes to a 'new animism'[1] and a 'new materialism'[2] without the metaphysical baggage of vitalism or neo-vitalism. Lucretius did not give us mathematical formulas or experimental data, but he did give us the best account he could of the *kinetic* nature of things.

He also developed an exciting approach to *writing history*. Instead of laying out *a priori* principles of history or attributing his ignorance to the 'randomness' of nature, Lucretius created what we might call a '*process philosophy of history*'. Instead of laws, Lucretius focused on *tendencies* and *emergent patterns*. His fascinating kinetic history is one of vortices, mean-ders, dendrites, and interwoven cycles.

This chapter looks at the material evidence Lucretius offers for the death of the world and what this tells us about nature, history, philosophy, and ethics. Specifically, I want to look closely at lines 5.235–508.

Everything Flows through the Doors of Death

If elements (earth, air, fire, and water) make up the world, and these elements are 'perishable bodies' [*mortali corpore*] (5.238), then the world itself is made of perishable bodies and is therefore perishable (5.235–9).

> *Principio quoniam terrai corpus et umor*
> *aurarumque leves animae calidique vapores,*
> *e quibus haec rerum consistere summa videtur,*
> *omnia nativo ac mortali corpore constant,*
> *debet eodem omnis mundi natura putari,*

> To begin first, since the body belonging to the earth and water
> and the light breath of the airy breezes and hot heat,
> from which this sum of things is seen to be put together,
> all consist of a body which has been born and is mortal, the whole
> nature of the world should be thought to consist of the same body.

It is essential to draw a critical distinction between 'the world' and 'nature' for Lucretius. The world [*mundi*] is a moving and open com-posite of things. Nature is the *material process* by which the world came into being and will pass away. This is not an ontological dualism. Nature is fully immanent with the historical creation and destruction of the world, like a tapestry of things woven from folded threads of matter, as discussed in Book I.[3]

Since all the bodies that compose the world have been drawn out [*figuris*] by the first threads of matter (5.241), they will also be unmade. This is because nature is a *process* and not a permanent form, substance, or essence. By definition, it tends to spread out and dissipate itself. Even time and space will dissolve.

Lucretius urges us to take a look at the integrated and iterative cycles all around us. Rocks and minerals are roasted by the sun, ground up by feet, and blown up as dust into the clouds and air (5.251–4). This dirt then rains back down and creates new earth. In this way, 'the earth is diminished and grows and increases again', as part of the rock cycle (5.260). Similarly, water continually flows from springs and rivers because it is replenished by rain that has been 'unwoven' [*retexens*] from lakes and rivers by the rays of the sun (5.267). This is the water cycle. The air, Lucretius says, is filled with 'whatever flows off of things' [*quod cumque fluit de rebus*] (5.275) and is thus constantly mutating [*mutatur*] its form and content in a feedback loop with everything else (5.275–80).

> . . . *qui nisi contra*
> *corpora retribuat rebus recreetque fluentis*
> *omnia iam resoluta forent et in aëra versa.*
> *haut igitur cessat gigni de rebus et in res*
> *reccidere, adsidue quoniam fluere omnia constat.*

> . . . Unless it gave
> back bodies to things again and renewed them as they flowed,
> all would by now have been dissolved and turned into air.
> Not at all then does air stop coming from things and falling
> back into things, since it is certain that everything is constantly in flux.

Unless the air gave back to things what they had evaporated or released in some way, everything would have dissolved already. Iterative and material cycles stabilise the constant dissipation of matter and motion. One remarkable consequence of this is that since matter is constantly 'flowing off' things and returning to them, they are never strictly identical with themselves. Nothing is what it is. This is not a metaphysical point that Lucretius merely assumes. It is a deduction from the sensuous observation of nature. Since everything on earth is continually undergoing cycles, it means that 'it is certain that everything is constantly in flux'.

Lucretius' philosophy of history is one of material processes and not of self-identical subjects or objects. All that is solid is continually melting into the air as heat, and returning as something else. Matter is fundamentally indeterminate. It cannot be said to 'be', 'not be', 'both be and not be', or 'neither be nor not be'. The language of 'being' is strictly inadequate to describe historical processes. Since we often fill history with subjects and objects, Lucretius proposes a real shift in our thinking.

Even the 'liquid fountain of light' [*liquidi fons luminis*] that pours out from the sun comes into being, perishes, and is replenished in a cycle of creation and destruction. However, since all cycles tend towards dissipation, Lucretius concludes that the cycle of light from our sun and all the stars in the sky will extinguish itself.

Most radically, Lucretius says that everything that entwines, encircles, and encompasses the earth is perishable as well (5.318–23).

> *Denique iam tuere hoc circum supraque quod omnem*
> *continet amplexu terram: si procreat ex se*
> *omnia, quod quidam memorant, recipitque perempta,*
> *totum nativo ac mortali corpore constat;*
> *nam quodcumque alias ex se res auget alitque,*
> *deminui debet, recreari, cum recipit res.*

> Next, now gaze at that which is above and surrounds the whole
> earth in its woven embrace. If it brings forth everything
> from itself, as some relate, and takes them back when they perish,
> then the entirety of it exists with a body that was born and will die.
> For whatever makes other things grow and nourishes them from itself
> must be diminished, and be restored when it receives things back.

Air surrounds the earth, but with our gaze we can also see the heavens and stars [*aether*] that surround the whole earth [*amplexu terram*] (3.319). Lucretius describes aether in very similar language elsewhere as a 'woven embrace' of the planet [*complexu quem tenet aether*] (2.1066). Since he has just described the perishable cycles of air, he turns now to discuss the perishable nature of the entire heavens.

The rest of the unlimited nature of the cosmos surrounds the earth. 'Some relate' that the earth emerged from the aether, but, for Lucretius, the aether itself came from the even more primary 'first beginnings' [*geni-*

talis origo] (5.176) that preceded all the elements. If the earth was born from the larger cosmos and is nourished by it, it will return to the cosmos. Like every material cycle, the aether cycle tends towards dissipation. The material aether that weaves its embrace around the earth will also one day perish. What we today call 'outer space' came into being and will die. As Lucretius described in earlier books, space and time are not *a priori* universal features of nature. They are emergent properties of nature's 'indeterminate' swerving, which occurs '*incerto tempore ferme incertisque locis spatio*' (2.218–19). As such, space and time, too, will perish in the fires of history.

Only indeterminate matter will not perish. This is because it is not a self-identical thing but an 'indivisible material' [*solida cum corpore*] *process* or flow (5.552). Things [*rerum*] can unravel because they are woven threads [*ordia*], but the threads themselves are processes and cannot dissolve. A flow of matter is never identical to itself. It has an indeterminate and unlimited being and thus cannot '*be*' destroyed.

Similarly, the universe itself as a process of processes is continually fleeing and surpassing itself. Matter suffers no blows or turbulence because *it is the swerving turbulence* that forms things first. Motion is what allows things to emerge and perish in history, but the process of arising and dying itself cannot perish or become 'unwoven' [*dissoluique*] (5.360). Nature is thus not divided from itself such that it could then break itself apart.[4]

Everything woven from the threads of matter will perish because matter is always in motion. Processes are open and continually crossing borders. As such, they are always beginning and ending, like the Roman god Janus referenced by Lucretius at 5.373–5.

haud igitur leti praeclusa est ianua caelo
nec soli terraeque neque altis aequoris undis,
sed patet immani et vasto respectat hiatu.

Therefore the door of death is not shut for the heavens,
nor for the sun, earth, nor the towering waves of the ocean,
but it stands open and waits with its monstrous and vast chasm.

Janus was a god of passage, transition, process, and motion. He presided over beginnings and endings at the same time without contradiction. Even the stars and heavens [*caelo*] (5.373) pass through the doors of death and destroy themselves by passage.

Figure 3.1 A statue of the Roman god Janus. Janus is traditionally depicted as having two faces, one looking to the past and the other to the future. Wikimedia Commons.

A World of (Im)balanced Strife

Everything flows and cycles. Earth, air, fire, and water all undergo a continual transformation of themselves through their cycles of creation and destruction. Furthermore, each is continually torn apart and merged with the others in what Lucretius calls the 'breath of balanced strife' [*spirantes aequo certamine*] (5.392).

> *tantum spirantes aequo certamine bellum*
> *magnis inter se de rebus cernere certant,*

So great a war do they breathe out in their balanced contest
as they struggle among themselves to come to a decision about great
things,

For Lucretius, natural history is neither harmonious cooperation according to a divine plan, nor is it competition over scarce resources in a world of randomness. The 'great members' [*membra*] or elements of nature continually destroy and rebuild themselves and one another *through one another*, and *as one another*. This is not homeo*stasis* or equilibrium but a homeo*rhesis*, far-from-equilibrium, from the Greek word and goddess *rhea*, meaning 'flow'.

The world is a metastable fluid-dynamic process akin to breathing [*spirantes*]. It is an iterative and woven [*exordia*] (5.331) process that takes in and pushes out. With each breath, something dies and something is reborn. The inhalation of the universe is a syncopated rhythm rippling through everything large and small. It experiments and makes vast decisions that take form in undulating patterns that shape galactic spirals, planetary orbits, and water cycles. Nature weaves and unweaves [*retexens*] elements (5.389).

This 'breathing balance of strife' is neither mechanically determined in advance nor random, Lucretius says (5.416–21).

Sed quibus ille modis coniectus materiai
fundarit terram et caelum pontique profunda,
solis lunai cursus, ex ordine ponam,
nam certe neque consilio primordia rerum
ordine se suo quaeque sagaci mente locarunt
nec quos quaeque darent motus pepigere profecto,

But in what ways this throwing-together of matter laid
the foundations of the earth, sky, and the vast depths of the sea,
and the courses of the sun and moon, I will weave into place.
For certainly not by design did these first threads of things
weave themselves together with knowing intelligence,
nor surely did they reach an agreement about what motions each would
   take.

World history was 'thrown together by matter' [*coniectus materiai*] (5.416). The world is not a static assemblage but a moving *conjection*. It is neither subject nor object, but a *conject* or a mutating rhythm. The first threads [*primordia*] (5.419) did not weave [*ordine*] (5.420) themselves into place following any blueprint, design, or fixed natural laws. They do not have any *specific* goal or telos that they are trying to attain. As Virginia Woolf wrote in her novel *The Waves*, 'To speak of knowledge is futile. All is experiment and adventure. We are forever mixing ourselves with unknown quantities.'[5]

Matter is not passive or stupid, but that does not mean that it has a 'knowing intelligence' [*sagaci mente*] that knows in advance what nature will necessarily do. This is, in part, because the movement of matter is 'constantly swerving' [*declinare solerent*] and 'indeterminate' [*incerto*]. If nature moved randomly, nothing would hold together for very long. In nature, one movement follows another, responding to another, iterating without ever strictly repeating anything. History is an intelligence in nature, but it does not know in advance, but only experimentally.

The movement of the first threads [*primordia*] (5.422), Lucretius says, is 'sewn together' [*consuerunt*] (5.424) in many ways into many unions [*multa modis multis . . . coetus*] (5.422–6). From this process, 'larger unions are woven together' [*magnarum rerum fiunt exordia saepe*] (5.430). However, as matter 'experiments' with its indeterminate motions [*motus experiundo*], (5.428) it also tends to 'spread out' [*volgata*] (5.427). Thermodynamically, larger conjunctions such as dendrites and vortices tend to increase the rate of energetic dissipation or 'spreading out'. Certain conjunctions help spread things out faster than an evenly paced dissolution.

A Strange Storm

Why is the world dying? The world is dying because it was born from a material indeterminacy that found a way to dissipate itself through the iterative turbulence of a 'strange storm', Lucretius says. Before the sun, stars, sea, earth, air, light, or any 'thing' [*rerum*] 'resembling' [*similus*] (5.435) things we know, there was a 'strange, extraordinary, and novel storm' from which the first threads [*primordia*] were stirred [*coorta*] into a 'huge shapeless heap' [*molesque*] (5.436). In this formless and metamorphic heap, 'all kinds' [*omnigenis*] of motion [*motus*], spacing [*intervalla*], pathways [*vias*], collisions [*plaga*], interweaving [*conexus*], and weight [*pondera*] were 'unravelled' [*discordia*] and 'run-together in a turbulent mixture of strife' [*concursus motus turbabat proelia miscens*] (5.437–9).

Lucretius is describing here an extraordinary situation. At the beginning of the universe, there was not nothing, void, space, time, or being. Instead, there were only *indeterminate material processes*. Nothing comes from nothing, so Lucretius says that, in the beginning, there was everything. However, it was everything in its purely indeterminate state of difference, so different from itself that there was no single determinate 'thing' [*rerum*]. This 'heap' was not 'different from' some other determinate thing, since no determinate thing yet existed. Matter 'existed' as a kind of positively charged indeterminate void of unwoven [*discordia*] threads. All determinate forms are emergent properties of this more primary ontological indeterminacy.

Lucretius says that this initial state of flux did not even resemble itself. It was a strange kind of anti-form that nature drew so variously and in so entangled a way that nothing resembled anything else [*dissimilis formas variasque figuras*]. In contrast to the quasi-theological idea of a self-identical infinite singularity at the start of the big bang, Lucretius describes a counter-form of indeterminate matter. Instead of being or non-being, Lucretius describes a *non-identity* or *strange becoming* at the beginning of the cosmos.

At present, there is no consensus among cosmologists about the universe before the moment of the big bang. However, Lucretius' description does prefigure the contemporary theory of indeterminate fluctuating quantum fields. The fluctuation of these fields gave rise to space, time, and the fourteen known fundamental quantum fields.[6]

Unsurprisingly, such a theory results in a radically different kind of cosmology and natural history than ones that start with the identity of being. Lucretius follows the consequences of this initial idea through celestial motions, evolution, and anthropology, up to his present. This is the historical journey I would like to take us on in this book.

The most immediate consequence of the history of the world, beginning with an indeterminate material process, is that there is no pregiven goal of the universe. If the cosmos began indeterminately, then it is free to dissipate and experiment. If the cosmos began with nothingness or unity (being), then we must assume an *ex nihilo* cause of its initial emergence and a pregiven totality of 'what is and can be'. However, if the universe is *indeterminate fluctuations*, then there cannot *be* a closed totality or a pregiven set of total ways it can dissipate.

So, first, there is indeterminate becoming, Lucretius says. Then, this strange storm begins to spread out, dissipate, and disperse [*diffugere*]

(5.443) through an emergent turbulent process into different spatial regions where the first threads are more or less entangled. Where they were more entangled [*perplexa*] there was more gravity or weight [*gravia*] (5.450). As space and matter became entangled, they concentrated and pulled away from lighter, less entangled threads.

Here again, Lucretius is ahead of his time with his materialist theory of gravity. One significant possible consequence of our current understanding of quantum entanglement is that space and time themselves are the results of woven relational processes. If this is the case, then there are not relations between *relata* in space and time, but space-time itself is fully relational, material, and emergent. This relational structure is also what contemporary 'entropic gravity theory' proposes.

At its core, the idea of entropic gravity is simple. In the quantum vacuum state of indeterminate fluctuations, the more the entanglement, the higher the entropy of a specific region. Thus, the measure of entropy in a given region, according to physicist Sean Carroll, 'turns out to be naturally proportional to the area of the region's boundary. The reason isn't hard to understand: field vibrations in one part of space are entangled with regions all over, but most of the entanglement is concentrated on nearby regions.'[7]

The higher the entanglement, the higher the entropy, and the closer the fluctuations are to one another. The weaker the entanglement, the more distant. Thus the laws of space-time in general relativity, according to this theory, emerge from entropic and entangled motion.[8] Gravity, in this theory, emerges from material kinetic entanglement similar to what Lucretius proposed. It has taken two thousand years, but some physicists have finally started to consider a materialist theory of gravity. We have finally caught up with Lucretius.

In quantum physics, processes make up objects, not the other way around. 'The world is in a ceaseless process of change', down to the most fundamental processes of matter and motion in quantum physics.[9] In some quantum gravity theories, indeterminate and relational quantum processes are even more fundamental than space and time itself. As the Italian physicist Carlo Rovelli writes,

We can think of the world as made up of *things*. Of *substances*. Of *entities*. Of something that *is*. Or we can think of it as made up of *events*. Of *happenings*. Of *processes*. Of something that *occurs*. Something that does not last, and that undergoes continual transformation, that is not permanent in time. The destruction of the notion of time in fundamental physics is the crumbling of the first of these two perspectives, not of the second. It is the realization of the ubiquity of impermanence, not of stasis in a motionless time.[10]

If quantum processes are genuinely fundamental, then even space and time are emergent properties of matter in motion. With all its stars, galaxies, and black holes, our entire universe unfolded itself from an indeterminately high energy region at the moment of the big bang. Before the big bang, there was no determinate space, time, matter, physical laws, or fundamental fields. However, there was not nothing either; there was an indeterministic state of flux. All that is came to be through *processes* and *patterns* of relational iteration.

Cosmic Volcanism

The earth is one entangled mass of matter with one kind of gravity, among others. When the earth was first forming, Lucretius says, weightier matters sank to the middle, and lighter ones worked their way up *through* the earth along passageways [*foramina*] (5.457) to the surface. Once they reached the surface, the more massive flows stayed on the surface, and the lighter ones left the planet. Just as we watch water evaporate from 'ever-flowing rivers' [*fluviique perennes*] into the 'sky and congeal into woven clouds' [*corpore concreto subtexunt nubila caelum*], so the earth breathes lighter matter [*exhalantque*] upwards (5.463–6).

This description is not only generally consistent with what we presently know about the formation of the earth; it is also something that we often forget. The earth is not a static foundation but a continually shifting ground filled with pores and tubes. It is continuously pouring out matter into the atmosphere and radiating the lightest matters such as heat and helium into space. The earth is not the only source of cosmic matter, but it does contribute.

The key idea is that the earth is a moving process that is slowly dissipating itself out into space. If we take this material idea seriously, it ought to change the way we think about philosophical 'foundations'. What if philosophy has based its quest for foundations on the false assumption that the earth itself is a solid ground? If the earth is our most immediate foundation for thought, what does it mean that it is mobile, shifting, becoming, degenerative, excessive, and generous? For Lucretius, the earth is, therefore, an anti-foundation, continually weaving and unweaving itself without a fixed identity.

The lightest matters of the cosmos [*aether*] then diffused and expanded outwards. They 'bent' [*flexit*] (5.468), 'enfolded' [*complexu*] (5.470), and wove [*exordia*] (5.471) an embrace around everything. Between the earth and these farther off regions, the spheres of the sun and moon formed, turned, and revolved as parts of the whole world (5.473–7). We should note well, however, that Lucretius gives this description of cosmic dissipation *for our planet*. We must also remember that, for Lucretius, the earth is not the only planet. There are an unlimited number of worlds in nature. If we wanted to follow out this turbulent and dissipative description of cosmic origin and volcanism, we would presumably want to do this for every world. However, since we only know our world, Lucretius describes its relationship to the broader universe here.

If we were to expand this idea, we would see a vision of many celestial bodies congealed into heavier and lighter weights or gravities. All of these are continually breaking themselves down through internal weight and heat and dissipating their lighter matters outwards through their circulation along celestial paths. Lucretius argued explicitly in Book I that there is no centre of the universe and that it is not a sphere (1.1053–69).

The idea of cosmic volcanism also fits his theory of simulacra in Book IV (4.42–62). There, Lucretius argued that flows of matter are continually radiating out of all things from inside them towards the periphery. Where these membranes [*membrana*] diffract with one another, they can produce new objects and images. Lucretius even uses the Latin word *membra* several times to describe the planets and cosmic bodies (5.244; 5.381; 5.445; 5.479). Since simulacra comprise all things, it follows that planets, stars, and moons would also be shedding their matters and producing new diffractive conjunctions throughout the cosmos.

Conclusion

Everything flows, and to flow is to move through the always-open doors of death. Unlike many historians, ancient and modern, Lucretius begins his history with the origins of the universe. By doing so, he must take a stand on the nature of nature itself and of world history. Although this seems far distant and even trivial to evolution and human history, it is not. Where we begin our history shapes our assumptions about what history is.

The bias of so many Western historians and philosophers has been to begin history with classical Greece. This has profoundly shaped their starting assumptions and limited their conclusions. Expanding history to early humans and Eastern cultures is better, but still not enough. The still current bias to start our histories with modern Western humanity is symptomatic of the division between the humanities and sciences that currently plagues academia. Humanists are often narrowly trained to read texts and constrain their inquiries to documents and leave the rest to scientists (archaeologists, palaeontologists, and anthropologists). In turn, scientists are often narrowly trained to gather data and thus often lack the interpretive and critical skills of humanists. New materialism in general and Lucretius, in particular, offer us an invitation to rethink the narrow starting points of our training to try to recover the interwoven character of knowledge.

The lines examined in this chapter on the mortality and death of the world begin the theory of historical materialism in such a way that historical narratives featuring progress, biocentrism, anthropocentrism, eternal laws, or secure eternal foundations of any kind are entirely out of the question. We live in a dying world whose general tendency is to iterate itself through dissipation as optimally as possible until death.

However, before we move on to look at the enormous consequences of Lucretius' cosmic history for evolution on earth, we need to turn briefly to the nature of celestial bodies, whose motions shape and express earth's history in profoundly important ways. Since the micro-cosmic iterates the macrocosmic, for Lucretius, this is a significant next move.

Notes

1 See Nurit Bird-David, '"Animism" Revisited: Personhood, Environment, and Relational Epistemology', *Cultural Anthropology*, 40.S1 (1999): S67–S91.

2 Christopher N. Gamble, Joshua S. Hanan, and Thomas Nail, 'What is New Materialism?', *Angelaki: Journal of the Theoretical Humanities*, 24.6 (2019): 111–34.

3 See Thomas Nail, *Lucretius I: An Ontology of Motion* (Edinburgh: Edinburgh University Press, 2018).

4 Thomas Nail, *Lucretius II: An Ethics of Motion* (Edinburgh: Edinburgh University Press, 2020), 108.

5   Virginia Woolf, *The Waves* (1931) (Orlando, FL: Harvest/Harcourt, 1959), 118.

6   See Carlo Rovelli, *The Order of Time*, trans. Erica Segre and Simon Carnell (New York: Riverhead Books, 2018).

7   See Sean Carroll, *Something Deeply Hidden: Quantum Worlds and the Emergence of Spacetime* (Boston: Dutton, 2019).

8   For more on a review of entropic gravity and its relationship to loop quantum gravity, see Lee Smolin, 'Newtonian Gravity in Loop Quantum Gravity', *Perimeter Institute for Theoretical Physics*, 29 October 2018, https://arxiv.org/pdf/1001.3668.pdf (accessed 12 July 2021).

9   Rovelli, *The Order of Time*, 97.

10 Rovelli, *The Order of Time*, 97.

4. It's a Turbulent Whirled

History is deep and is expressed mainly by the movement of cosmic bodies. What, then, is the structure and motion of the cosmos and its celestial bodies that has dominated history? What can this tell us about the nature of historical movement more generally? This is the question that Lucretius poses in lines 509–770 of Book V.

However, answering this question is one of the knottiest problems in the poem and marks a definite turning point. For the first time in the poem, Lucretius says at the start of Book V that no mortal can sing a poem about nature that does justice to its majesty. However, if the world itself is also mortal, as he has just argued, nothing in the world can sing the grandeur of nature. How is this possible?

Nothing in the world of things can represent or capture the majesty of nature because nature is not a thing. It is a *process* immanent to the world. The world is mortal because it is historical, and it is historical because nature is dissipative. A dying world cannot render a representation of the process of death itself. It can only *undergo* the process. The world can express and perform nature, but it cannot adequately describe what nature is. No objective account is possible because there is no outside of the world. The world is an expression of nature. It is the sensible trace of nature's flux.

What, then, is the practice of history? It is an exploratory step-by-step act or performance that *expresses* or *performs* nature. Lucretius cannot sing *about* nature's majesty, but he can *become* part of the grandeur of nature in the act of singing. This is precisely what he tries to do in these exemplary lines of Book V. Therefore, this chapter aims to study these lines carefully and show how they articulate the performative nature of history.

Sheep May Safely Graze

Instead of giving a single determinate account of why and how heavenly bodies move, Lucretius gives us several possible descriptions. Perhaps winds blow the whole sky, maybe the sky stays in place and the wind blows the stars, or perhaps everything roams around like sheep in search of food. This is the first time that Lucretius explicitly offers several competing accounts of things in his poem. This makes these passages in Book V challenging and strange to read. If he does not know the answer, why is he putting forward hypotheses? What does this practice tell us about the nature of his historical method?

The first reason for this approach, Lucretius says, is that history unfolds differently in different worlds. Multiple histories coexist alongside one another. Even today, we have seen only a small portion of the universe's history. If no fixed set of forms or processes limits the unfolding of matter, there can be no universal history. There is no single view from which we can understand the past. This is because history is not linear but diffractive and turbulent. It manifests itself differently in different worlds. Different historical processes intertwine with one another, and so we cannot reduce them to cause or effect, or to a single vision or vantage. The poet sings (5.526–33):

Nam quid in hoc mundo sit eorum ponere certum
difficile est; sed quid possit fiatque per omne
in variis mundis varia ratione creatis,
id doceo, plurisque sequor disponere causas,
motibus astrorum quae possint esse per omne;
e quibus una tamen siet hic quoque causa necessest
quae vegeat motum signis; sed quae sit earum
praecipere haudquaquamst pedetemptim progredientis.

For to assert as certain which of these is true in this world
is difficult, but what can and what does happen throughout the universe
in different worlds brought forth in different ways,
this I teach and am proceeding to set out the many causes
which are able to exist for the motions of the stars throughout the universe.
Yet one of these must be the cause also in our world
that imparts movement to the constellations; but which of these it is
is not at all to declare for one who is progressing step by step.

If matter is 'constantly swerving' [*declinare solerent*] (2.221) 'indeterminately' [*incerto*] (1.181), and 'everything is in constant flux' [*fluere omnia constat*] (5.280) and 'motion' [*omnia migrant*] (5.830), then how can we possibly have a 'certain' [*certum*] (5.526) knowledge of how things came to be, much less all the possible ways things could have come to be?

Here Lucretius encounters a fundamental indeterminacy at the heart of history. 'Different worlds emerged through different logics of creation' [*variis mundis varia ratione creatis*] (5.528). In the same universe [*omne*] (5.527), different historical logics can be at work simultaneously. The history of our world is different from the history of others. Nature is different from itself and proceeds as it goes experimentally, without any fixed plan or *a priori* laws. Everything creatively emerges because it began indeterminately.

How can we know with 'certainty' which historical path our world took to get to where we are now? Furthermore, if each history itself is indeterminate swerving, how can we trace a history with no single local 'cause'? Instead of providing only one history, Lucretius proposes several histories simultaneously. He gives us a pluralist history that enacts the method of the universe.[1]

The second reason Lucretius gives for his 'uncertain or indeterminate' [*incerto*] historical account is that he is 'progressing step by step' [*pedetemptim progredientis*] (5.533). The poet is our guide and takes us on an 'experimental, tentative, and sensuous' [*tendō*] stroll with his 'feet' [*ped*]. He walks along ahead of us, experimenting and trying out theories just as nature does. Lucretius gives us a performative history of the present. There is no determinant plan in advance and no goal at the end. Instead, one motion follows searchingly after another. Like the process of history itself, Lucretius 'spreads' [*tendo*] out on his stroll, with each step responding creatively to what came before. This is not the method of universal history proposed by earlier Greek philosophers.

Of particular interest is Lucretius' third account of the movement of the stars [*motum signis*] (5.532). He compares the movement of the heavens to the meandering of serpents and sheep (5.523–5).

> . . . *sive ipsi serpere possunt*
> *quo cuiusque cibus vocat atque invitat euntis,*
> *flammea per caelum pascentis corpora passim.*

                                        . . . or whether they themselves
can creep wherever their food calls and invites them as they go,
feeding their flaming bodies this way and that through the heavens.

This description of the stars' movement also invokes Lucretius' earlier
description of roaming sheep seen at a distance at the start of Book II
(2.317–19).

> *nam saepe in colli tondentes pabula laeta*
> *lanigerae reptant pecudes quo quamque vocantes*
> *invitant herbae gemmantes rore recenti,*
> *et satiati agni ludunt blandeque coruscant;*
> *omnia quae nobis longe confusa videntur*
> *et velut in viridi candor consistere colli,*

For often on the hillside, cropping their glad pastures,
wool-bearing flocks creep on wherever the grass, sparkling
with fresh dew, calls out and invites each of them,
and the lambs, now full, play and gently butt their heads.
All these things appear blurred to us from a distance,
and stand still like a white blotch on a green hillside.

By comparing the two kinds of movement, Lucretius draws a sublime
connection between the macroscopic motion of the heavens and the
relatively microscopic movement of sheep, as seen from a distance. The
sheep spread out over the grass like reptiles, as their food calls them,
'*reptant . . . vocantes invitant . . .*' (2.317–19), just as the stars spread out like
snakes called and invited by their food, '*serpere . . . vocat . . . invitat . . .*'
(5.523–5).

This pattern of motion tells us something about the process of history
more broadly. From stars to sheep, nature tends to *spread out* [*reptant/
serpere*] at every scale. Nature tends to seek out its unravelling [*dissolvere*]
and dissolution through an active search to dissipate more energy. Each
consumption increases dissipation and hastens the unravelling of the universe. Nature abhors all energy gradients, and so high concentrations 'call
out and invite' dissipation into lower ones. The spiralling snake's image is
perfect for the spiralled, vortical, and turbulent motions that accompany
the energetic dissolution of matter at every scale through history.

Like all other energy processes, the stars in the sky were born, eat,
and will perish. The blurry white stars, like the blurry white sheep,
are seen at a distance to move around the universe, consuming matter

and burning themselves out. Stars and sheep are not programmed in advance but rather respond creatively and with unique movements to their energetic milieu by roaming, experimenting, playing. History is no different. Water pools in low areas and green grass grows after it rains, just as dense stars attract smaller ones until they explode, and others consume them. Energy flows, matter cycles, and everything dissipates.

History is the experimentation of nature, step by step, listening and responding, just as the poet proceeds, listening carefully, and singing back with tentative [*tendo*] experiments of his own. Lucretius says he is like a bee wandering through the mountains of the Muses looking for new springs and new flowers (3.11). The poet is searching the hills for new sensations to make his mind bloom like a flower, just as the sheep hear the call of new grassy energy gradients. Lucretius feeds on vegetation, and his mind unfurls like a blooming flower with a *vision* of nature (1.920–34).

Philosophical knowledge is, therefore, not unlike nature. It is not absolute but tentative, experimental, proceeding bit by bit in search of new gradients and previously unthought gaps between the known and unknown. Philosophy is just as speculative and dissipative as the stars and the sheep in search of their gradients. At the limits of sensation, things appear blurry at a distance. Nonetheless, they call out and invite us to listen and think about them.

According to Lucretius, the cosmos spreads out like the 'limbs' [*membra*] of an octopus in search of nourishment and play. The stars and planets are outstretched searching limbs or tentacles, searching out new pleasures and new methods of dissipation and iteration.

Summanus: The Dying God

The dark and turbulent nature of celestial motion in the temple of Summanus is significant here (5.520–1). Summanus, the Roman god of the skies, storms, lightning, and thunder *at night*, was also the dark brother of Jupiter. Thus, he was akin to the Greek chthonic gods of destruction, dissipation, and death, Poseidon and Hades.

quaerentesque viam circum versantur et ignes
passim per caeli volvunt summania templa;

and seeking an exit turn round and roll the stars/constellations
through the temple of Summanus in the sky.

Figure 4.1 Minoan clay bottle showing an octopus, 1500 BCE. Wikimedia
Commons.

The importance of invoking Summanus here is that motion, turbulence,
and lightning play an essential role in the dissipation and death of the
earth. The world is dying because it was born into Jupiter's light, and
Jupiter also has a darker brother. The dual nature of the sky is a crucial
aspect of myth but also of cosmology more generally.[2]

There is, as Empedocles says, a 'twofold' aspect to nature in which
creation and destruction are two aspects of the same process or movement. Lightning is one of the most potent non-organic dissipators of

Figure 4.2 Group of ancient roman statues of Persephone (as Isis), Cerberus, and Pluto (as Serapis), from Gortys. Wikimedia Commons.

energy on earth per area. Its branching dendrites and awe-inspiring light, especially at night, give us a striking visual image of a basic pattern of history. History experiments dendritically, just like lightning. It spreads out, searching for the most optimal path to dissipate the gradient between sky and earth.

The temple of Summanus is a vision of a death-bound cosmos. The earth destroys itself but leaves a trace of its death in the sky as a message. The world will die just like this. The stars that now circulate through the temple of Summanus will all perish along the same dissipative route. The heavens iterate and circulate like the 'rolling rapids' [*volvunt; rapidi*] (5.519–21), but in doing so, they pass through a turbulent temple of dissipation and must dissipate. It is precisely the rolling, turning rapidity of turbulence that increases the dissolution of matter.

Woven From the Same Roots

The earth dissipates the sky, and the sky, in turn, dissipates the earth. The weaving and unweaving of the world is a mutually transformative affair. The earth dissipates itself through 'rolling rapids' of air. As it moves, its 'mass gradually dissipates and vanishes' [*evanescere paulatim et descrescere pondus*] (5.535–6), evaporating into the air. The earth sits in the middle of its airy waste, surrounded [*media mundi regione*] (5.534) like the material souls of humans.

Lucretius never definitively says that the earth is either spherical or flat.[3] He says that the sun and moon are spheres and that the earth hangs in the middle of the atmosphere, surrounded. He says that it is 'possible' that the sun is extinguished at night and rekindled in the morning (5.650–704). This could be true only relative to a group of observers on a round earth or, Lucretius is prepared to admit, this may not be what happens. He also says that the earth's *conical* shadow 'may' eclipse the moon (5.762–70).[4] However, the shadow could be conical whether the earth was flat or round. In short, Lucretius ventures many hypotheses on celestial dynamics, but he is also explicit that he does not know for sure which ones are correct. As such, he is not philosophically committing to or compromised by these celestial speculations. The real value of his account lies elsewhere.

Just as human bodies and souls are 'woven' [*nexam*] throughout their entire body (3.217), the earth and the sky emerged from the same turbulent material process. The earth and sky are 'implanted and ingrafted' [*insita*] (5.538) into one another and sown together with 'common roots' [*communibus radicibus*] (5.554). The air is just a thinner version of the earth, which emerged through the earth's dissipation. Lucretius rejects the hard ontological division between the earth and the sky and avoids any kind of transcendence. Instead, he posits both as degrees of the same turbulent process, what David Abrams calls 'EAIRTH'.[5] The sky is the earth's breath. Earth's atmosphere is the product of its early volcanic activity and is deeply 'conjoined' [*coniuncta*] (5.558) to it.

Here again, Lucretius gives us a beautiful image of order woven from dissipation across several scales at once. The human body, soul, and limbs [*membra*] (5.540) are woven together just as the earth and sky are 'engrafted' together like the roots of plants. Some commentators interpret Lucretius' comparison of the earth with the human as an anthropocentric projection on to the earth. However, it is precisely the opposite. The human body has soul and breath precisely because the earth already created its breath and soul in the atmosphere. The human body has limbs only because the earth itself already created the limbs of the sky, plants, and animals. The human body and mind have the structure they do only because the earth had the same basic structure.

It is quite clear, for Lucretius, that humans follow in the image of the earth because the earth was first. To suggest otherwise is the real anthropocentrism. Humans are not separate enough from the earth such that they could project their being on to it. We do not live *on* earth. We *are* the earth and the sky. Lucretius wants us to remember and to feel the immanence of our bodies with the material world. Our thinking, feeling, and histories are not *about* the earth but are *expressions* of the dying earth. Inspired by Lucretius, Karl Marx wrote profoundly that 'In history as in nature, decay is the laboratory of life.'[6]

Material souls and limbs are iterative features of nature. They are the extensions, protrusions, and tentacles of a dissipative universe spreading out in all directions. The soul, for Lucretius, is not immaterial. This is the complete opposite account from the one Plato gives in the *Timaeus*. There is no craftsman and there is no ideal blueprint. A material soul moves immanently through the universe as a cosmic gas or dust. The heavenly bodies are the limbs of an active and creative cosmos. In this way, Lucretius retains all the dynamic creativity of the 'cosmic animal' with none of its Platonic idealism.

When air moves, it can also move the earth (through erosion and storms), and when the earth moves through earthquakes, its vibrations can cause tsunamis and thunderstorms in the air (5.550–1). Earth and sky touch and move one another closer to death because both are material. They mutually dissipate the energy of the other through the turbulent motion of the other – *as the other*.

Whirls and Cycles

The entire cosmos whirls and cycles. Dissipation produces iteration, and iteration increases dissipation. Here again, the spiral meander re-emerges as an image ahead of its time. In contrast to the perfect circular orbits befitting the immortal gods, Lucretius, following Democritus, suggests that the sun and moon are 'turbulent whirls' [*turbine*] (5.624).[7] Like the rest of nature, the heavens do not move in perfect eternal patterns but in unstable whirls that fluctuate and swerve.

Figure 4.3 Minoan clay cups with spiral decoration, Myrtoy-Pyrgos, Crete, 1500–1450 BCE. Wikimedia Commons.

Lucretius is not sure exactly how big the stars are or how big the sun and moon are, although he guesses (wrongly) that they are not very different from how they appear (5.586). But this is not what is most important to him, and he is readily open to correction on this point and others. However, most importantly, his method is based on sensation, experimentation, and trying things out 'step by step'. This is the material structure of history and thus of natural science. Science did not invent the experimental method but iterates what it finds in natural history. The three main points that are most important for Lucretius are that the heavens are not immortal gods, that the world is dissipative/iterative, and that history is turbulent.

This is a radical gesture well ahead of its time. The relationship between the sun, the earth, and the moon was the first 'three-body problem' in physics. Issac Newton, Galileo Galilei, Jean le Rond d'Alembert, and many others attempted to predict the sun's, earth's, and moon's trajectories based on the known laws of motion and failed. Eventually, Henri Poincaré proved that the periodicities between the three bodies were non-linear and *never repeated paths precisely*. There is no single solution to the collective movement of three bodies because they form an open system in which the third body alters slightly the course of the other two, which then changes the course of the third, which then modifies the other two, and so on. Therefore, nature proceeds 'step by step' without repeating itself, just as Lucretius' poem tries to.

The orbital motion of *all* the planets forms an open system without a single solution, only iterative paths. There are not just three bodies in the universe but a multiplicity. Classical mechanics was always a fantasy, and had we read Lucretius more carefully, we would have known this all along. Even the fastest computers in the world can only approach the 'three or more body' problems without solving them completely. Lucretius had already come to the general conclusion centuries before that celestial orbits are fully relational, iterative, and turbulent. They are woven together, engrafted, implanted systems full of turbulence, feedback, and dissipation. They are *whirling* cycles [*turbine*] (5.624), which never repeat but creatively iterate as they dissipate.

Night and Day

What is the nature of day and night? In this breathtaking passage, Lucretius provides a magnificent description of day and night that highlights a central theme of his entire cosmology and philosophy of nature. Nature weaves a web [*exordia*] that alternates between creation and destruction, birth and death. Nature goes down [*katabasis*] and comes back up again [*anabasis*] in loops and folds like a tapestry. Day and night are one of the many expressions of this cosmic rhythm, which tends towards dissipation.

Night 'buries and covers over' [*obruit*] day like a 'thick dark atmospheric blanket' [*caligine*] as the sun winds its whirling journey in orbit 'around and beneath the earth' [*sub terras cursum convortere*] (5.650–5). Night is depicted here as a kind of burial shroud woven around the earth. The heavens pass through the temple of Summanus and die. Then, in this next passage, something incredible happens (5.656–62).

Tempore item certo roseam Matuta per oras
aetheris auroram differt et lumina pandit,
aut quia sol idem, sub terras ille revertens,
anticipat caelum radiis accendere temptans,
aut quia conveniunt ignes et semina multa
confluere ardoris consuerunt tempore certo,
quae faciunt solis nova semper lumina gigni;

> Likewise in a certain rhythm Matuta scatters rosy
> dawn along the shores of ether and pours forth light,
> either because the same sun, returning beneath the earth,
> grabs the sky beforehand and tries to ignite it with its rays,
> or because fires gather together and many seeds
> of heat are accustomed to flow together at a fixed time,
> which always make the new light of the sun come into being

The critical point here, for Lucretius, is not whether the stars and sun die each night or precisely how they move. The key idea is that the stars, including the sun, move and die, and cycle no matter what. They go down and come back up. They iterate and dissipate like everything else in the world.

Most important is that the turning and swerving journey [*cursum convortere*] (5.655) of night and day is part of a much broader material process that orders our natural being and the history of all things. 'For we see much that happens rhythmically in all things' [*certo quae tempore*] (5.669). Trees, flowers, human growth and death, the seasons, and weather patterns all share in this same cosmic rhythm (5.677–9). This idea is not original to Lucretius, of course. It was the core of most prehistoric religions as far back as we are aware.[8] Everything in nature participates in a grand process of creation and destruction. Only with the rise of civilisations was this idea surpassed by eternal gods, unchanging forms, and other idealist abstractions.

Lucretius aims to give voice again to this suppressed mythopoetic and materialist tradition with an important twist. Everything is not only part of a process of creation and destruction, but this process also tends towards destruction because matter swerves indeterminately (5.677–9).

> *namque ubi sic fuerunt causarum exordia prima*
> *atque ita res mundi cecidere ab origine prima,*
> *conseque quoque iam redeunt ex ordine certo.*

> For since the first woven web of relations were thus
> and things have so fallen from the first origin of the world,
> following one after another they even now return in rhythmic order.

Why is there day and night, according to Lucretius? Because matter, since before the world, flows (falls) and *swerves* indeterminately. If matter were entirely subject to the deterministic bonds of fate [*foedera fati*], it would never have swerved or turned, and nothing in the world would have swerved or returned iteratively. Rhythms emerge in nature because matter repeats with a difference. Precise repetitions destroy novelty as does the lack of routines. Therefore nothing, for Lucretius, can be genuinely determined or random. Matter proceeds by 'following, pursuing, attending' [*conseque*] (5.679) itself 'step by step' [*pedetemptim*] (5.533). Nothing is *a priori* about nature. Since everything is an emergent feature that is still emerging and changing, indeterminacy is the only *foedera naturai* (1.586).

The rhythms of night and day, spring and autumn, birth and death, wind and rain, exist because matter is in the habit of swerving [*declinare solerent*]. They are rhythmic habits of creation and destruction that 'tend or try to spread out' [*temptō*] *ped*etically, step by step: *ped* + *temptō* = *pedetemptim*.

Lucretius at Samothrace

Lucretius is aware of this broader material structure of nature and finds a beautiful and intricate way to invoke its deeply mystical and mythological history. Matter goes down below the earth [*sub terras*] (5.658) through the dark temple of the chthonic Summanus and then comes back up in the blooming fires [*accendere*] (5.659) of rosy *Mater Matuta*.

> *Tempore item certo roseam Matuta per oras*
> *aetheris auroram differt et lumina pandit,*

> Likewise in a certain rhythm Matuta scatters rosy
> dawn along the shores of ether and pours forth light,

The mythic figure of Matuta ties together all these passages and perhaps everything in Book V, so it is worth thinking about her relation to this diurnal scene. Mater Matuta was the Roman goddess of grain, birth, the sea, and dawn. The Romans based her on the Greek goddess Leucothea or Ino. Ino raised her sister Semele's son Dionysus when she was impregnated by Zeus then tricked by Hera and killed. 'Ino was a primordial Dionysian woman, nurse to the god and a divine maenad', as Carl Kerényi says.[9] However, Hera sought revenge against Ino as well and caused her husband Athamas to go mad and try to kill her. She escaped him only by jumping into the ocean and dying with her

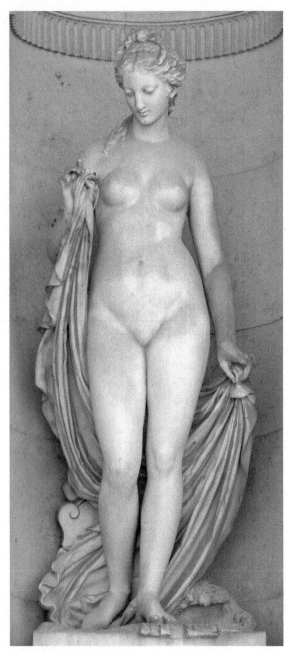

Figure 4.4 Jean Jules Allasseur, *Leucothea* (1862), south façade of the Cour Carrée in the Louvre, Paris. Wikimedia Commons.

son Melicertes. Zeus took pity on Ino and her son and made them both immortal ocean gods.

Ino was also associated with the Mysteries of Samothrace, which were second in importance only to the great Mysteries at Eleusis. Ino is said to have worn a purple veil, and thus the initiates into the Mystery were also girded with purple veils, which would protect them from death at sea.[10] The central figure among the largely chthonic gods who presided over the Mystery site was the great goddess. The goddess at Samothrace was also accompanied by lions, Minoan-style double axes, and spiral

Figure 4.5 Agamemnon, Talthybius, and Epeius, relief from Samothrace, c. 560 BCE. In Greek mythology, the Cabeiri were a group of enigmatic chthonic deities. They were worshipped in a Mystery cult at Samothrace. In this image we can also see the prehistoric Minoan spiral form on the right. Wikimedia Commons.

forms, suggesting that the ritual may have had its origins much earlier on Crete.[11]

The Mystery ritual structure at Samothrace and Eleusis followed the basic structure of the archaic fertility ritual. The mother goddess searches for her lost daughter; the daughter marries the dark god of the underworld, and then returns to the surface, with a baby boy.[12] These Mysteries were the basis of the oldest features of Greek religion. It was even Athenian law to purify burial sites by sowing grain to give the site back to the living.[13]

It is no coincidence that Ino appears in Homer's *Odyssey* as an ocean goddess who rescues Odysseus from the turbulent ocean storm brought on by Poseidon, the chthonic earth-shaker, to destroy him. Just as in the Mystery rituals, the goddess rises from the depths and tells Odysseus, her boy, not to fear death. Similarly, in Lucretius, the fear of death was the primary ethical focus of the Mystery religion. Ino gives Odysseus her woven veil to wrap around his waist, just as the initiates at Samothrace did, saying:

> 'Come, take this veil, and stretch it beneath thy breast. It is divine; there is no fear that thou shalt suffer aught or perish. But when with thy hands thou hast laid hold of the land, loose it from thee, and cast it into the wine-dark sea far from the land, and thyself turn away.' So saying, the goddess gave him the veil, and herself plunged again into the surging deep, like a diving bird; and the dark wave hid her . . . 'Woe is me! Let it not be that some one of the immortals is again weaving [*huphaínō*] a net to trap me, that she bids me leave my raft.' (*Odyssey*, 5.345–57)

Ino has a woven veil just as the great mother goddess weaves the world. If Odysseus is going to survive, he must also weave the veil around himself through the world's turbulent waves. However, once he reaches the shores of light, out of the ocean of death, the veil must return to the underworld's depths. Odysseus thus undergoes a journey of purification and initiation through the watery depths of death and returns to the shores of life like Ino's foster-son Dionysus.

Ino emerges from the sea's depths with a woven veil of life that Odysseus rightly worries is also a woven [*huphaínō*] veil of death – a cunning trap [*dolon*]. Life is woven from death and death from life by cunning, trickery, ensnarement, and entanglement. To be entangled in one is to be implicated in the other. This is the truth of the great Mystery at Samothrace. Every initiate to the cult, which meant almost

Neptune excite une tempête, qui brise le bâtiment d'Ulysse: Leucothée donne son voile à ce prince pour le sauver du naufrage.

Figure 4.6 Neptune stirs up a storm, which wrecks the ship of Odysseus; Leucothea gives her veil to the prince to save him from the shipwreck. Wikimedia Commons.

every Greek and Roman, knew this. Ino's veil is the woven web of nature.

Returning to Lucretius' Mater Matuta, we can now see the greater and more crucial mythological-naturalist scene. The oldest Mystery cults at the heart of Greek and Roman religion provide an aesthetic form of knowledge of the core material processes that order the entire universe, including the heavens, earth, plants, animals, and the weather. Matuta is the iterative interval and rhythm [*tempore*] (5.656) of nature. She stretches out her veil in creation and retracts it back in destruction like the blossoming flowers on the trees and the blossoming rose colour of the dawn stretching across the sky. She weaves and spreads [*differt*] her veil around the earth, disturbing and dissipating [*differt*] it at the same time (5.657).

Ino helps Odysseus reach shore just as Lucretius says Matuta reaches the shore [*oras aetheris*] (5.656–7). Her fires ascend from *katabasis* and 'spread, test, and feel' their way into the sky gradually [*temptans*], just as Lucretius walks and sings step by step [*pedetemptim*]. Matuta 'pours out light' [*lumina pandit*] (5.657) in a rhythmic order like the Minoan mother goddess Rhea, whose name means 'to flow', and who stands atop the sacred Mt Ida on Crete.[14] Water and light flow down from the 'mountain mother', 'mother goddess of Ida', or 'Idaean Mother'. Lucretius is speaking of the Phrygian Mt Ida, which the Romans named after the Mt Ida on Crete and dedicated to the Roman *Magna Mater deorum Idaea* or 'great Idaean mother of the gods'.[15] Mt Ida on Crete housed the cave where Rhea gave birth to Zeus. Mt Ida is the material and visionary source from which creation appears as a gathering of diverse flows of seeds [*semina multa confluere*] (5.660–1) sprouting up and blooming [*roseam*] (5.656).

Therefore, Lucretius gives us a materialist and naturalist framework that weaves together the natural patterns of the cosmos with the mythopoetic and archaic knowledge of those patterns. In Lucretius' reconstruction, Matuta/Rhea/Demeter is a goddess of swerving flows. She is the cyclical curvature of light and dark around the earth and the curving light of the lunar phases (5.731–6). She is also a swerving goddess in the sense that Demeter resists or swerves the will of Zeus and the *foedera fati* of the other gods who decided to let Hades abduct her daughter, Persephone. Against her fate and the tyranny of male domination, Demeter revolts and stops grain and springs from 'flowing' [*rheo*]. Eventually, she forces the gods to return Persephone to her. The mother also swerves in the historical sense that she splits off from herself into a daughter who dies and is reborn under various names.[16]

Matter, for Lucretius, flows and cycles through iterations of creation and destruction, each time introducing novelties that escape the cycle and spread out to dissipate the world. Lucretius gives us what we could

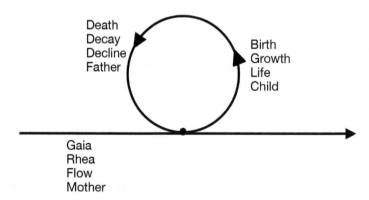

Figure 4.7 Kinomythology: the mother gives birth to a child who dies, goes to the underworld of the father, and is reborn. This is the Demeter, Persephone, Hades seasonal cycle.

call a 'kinetic mythology', 'kinomythics', or 'materialist mythology', different from animism, vitalism, or transcendence.

The Iterative Rhythms of Nature

Everything in nature happens in iterative rhythms. Lucretius deploys a version of the *Mystery triad* (mother, daughter, son/lover) to account for the 'certain rhythms' [*certo tempore*] (5.748) of the seasons. Spring begins with youthful Venus, Eros, Zephyr, and Flora, who 'covers [their path] completely with amazing colors and scents' (5.740). This vernal procession is followed by the mature mother, Ceres, and Calor (dry heat) and Aquilones (the north wind) in the summer. Then autumn and Bacchus [*Euhius Euan*] 'take steps' [*graditur*] together, followed by turbulent storms [*tempestates*], lightning, and the high winds of the south wind (Auster). 'High-thundering' Volturnus, too, comes and increases the turbulence of the earth. Finally, Bruma (winter solstice), followed by Hiemps (winter), comes with bitter cold.

The seasons move from life to death, from the warm winds to lightning, thunder, and bitter cold. The world is born and moves towards extinction. This trajectory is followed by Lucretius' poem, which begins with Venus and becomes increasingly attentive to turbulence, dissipation, and death as it walks onwards and downwards. The poem also mirrors the *katabasis* of the mother goddess into the underworld. Therefore, it is possible to read *De Rerum Natura* itself as a performative *katabasis*. It guides the reader through an initiation into the mystical materialism of a dying world of flows and folds.

Similarly, the moon runs through its monthly phases of light from full to empty (new). Lucretius concludes his speculative description of the heavens' movement, fittingly, with the poetic image of a solar eclipse. The world is born and will die, the day is born and covered with the night, and the stars come to be and pass away. All that is bright will become 'shrouded with darkness' (5.776). The movement of nature is like the large folding cloak that Demeter wears to mourn Persephone. Its twofold movement reveals and conceals simultaneously.

Conclusion

This is the big cosmic picture for Lucretius. The history of the world is dissipative and iterative. There can be no truly historical inquiry that ignores the nature of things and the iterative decline of the world. Nature cycles and unfolds itself into the cool darkness of space. The light of the stars, sun, and moon is in motion. It comes and goes. It is the material basis of the prehistoric myth of the triple moon goddess integrated over time into Greek religion under Hades, Dionysus, and others. Lucretius draws on this deep mythopoetic tradition, generalises it, and expands it into a theory of materialist naturalism.

Lucretius now turns to the more local history of the earth and the evolution of life. This is what I would like to look at more closely in the next chapter.

Notes

1 For a recent treatment, see R. J. Hankinson, 'Lucretius, Epicurus, and the Logic of Multiple Explanations', in Daryn Lehoux, A. D. Morrison, and Alison Sharrock (eds), *Lucretius: Poetry, Philosophy, Science* (Oxford: Oxford University Press, 2013), 69–97.

2 Georges Dumézil, *Myth et Epopée III: Histoires romaines* (Paris: Gallimard, 1981), part 2, ch. 3; Georges Dumézil, *Mitra-Varuna: essai sur deux representations indo-européennes de la souveraineté*, 2nd edn (Paris: Gallimard, 1948); Georges Dumézil, *La religione romana arcaica* (Milan: Rizzoli, 1977), 184 (*La religion romaine archaïque, avec un'appendice sur la religion des Étrusques* [Paris: Payot, 1964]).

3 Lee Fratantuono, *A Reading of Lucretius' De Rerum Natura* (London: Lexington Books, 2017), 342: 'Here the commentators lament that Lucretius never makes it explicit whether or not he views the world as a spherical globe or, for example, a flat disc. The poet's theory here is in some ways naïve and in other ways sophisticated.'

4 For a complete discussion of all the relevant passages, see Frederik A. Bakker, *Epicurean Meteorology: Sources, Method, Scope and Organization* (Leiden: Brill, 2016), 257–8.

5 Alan Atkisson, 'David Abrams: Breathing Ourselves Aware on Planet "Eairth"', *Alanatkisson.com*, 1 November 2010, https://alanat kisson.com/2010/11/01/david-abrams-breathing/ (accessed 12 July 2012).

6 Karl Marx, *Oeuvres: Economie I* (Paris: Gallimard, 1965), 955. This sentence appears only in the French version.

7 Empedocles thought that the sky rotates at high speed around the earth (A67), and he used the word *dinē* (B35.1). Rotation was fundamental for

the early atomists (Leucippus A1; Democritus A1); Democritus used the similar word *dînos*.

8   See Anne Baring and Jules Cashford, *The Myth of the Goddess: Evolution of an Image* (London: Arkana, 2000).

9   Carl Kerényi, *Dionysos: Archetypal Image of Indestructible Life*, trans. Ralph Manheim (Princeton: Princeton University Press, 1976).

10 'Already in 1951 Jeanmaire saw Leucothea as connected to the ritual immersion in the sea that precedes some Dionysiac ritual and mysteries, for example, those at Eleusis.' See Olga Levaniouk, 'Waters of the Underworld and Ino in the Odyssey', 2, https://www.academia.edu/37300274/Waters_of_the_Underworld_and_Ino_in_the_Odyssey_pdf (accessed 12 July 2012), citing H. Jeanmaire, *Dionysos: histoire du culte de Bacchus: l'orgiasme dans l'antiquité et les temps modernes, origine du théâtre en Grèce, orphisme et mystique dionysiaque, évolution du dionysisme aprè Alexandre* (Paris: Payot, 1951), 208–10. 'A scholiast to Apollonius of Rhodes 1.917 says that the mystai at Samothrace were saved at sea and that Odysseus is initiated and uses Leucothea's veil in place of the customary purple sash: Leucothea's kredemnon is reminiscent of the Samothracian sashes . . .' Levaniouk, citing Walter Burkert, *Greek Religion; Archaic and Classical*, trans. John Raffan (Malden, MA: Blackwell Publishing, 1985), 267; see also N. Lewis, 'Scholiast Parisina to Apollonius Rhodius 1.917', in *Samothrace 1: Ancient Literary Sources* (New York: Pantheon, 1959), http://scholarblogs.emory.edu/samothraciannetworks/the-ritual-promise/literary-texts/#ApolloniusScholia2 (accessed 20 May 2015).

11 Mark L. Lawall, '"In the Sanctuary of the Samothracian Gods": Myth, Politics, and Mystery Cult at Ilion', in Michael B. Cosmopoulos (ed.), *Greek Mysteries: The Archaeology of Ancient Greek Secret Cults* (London: Routledge, 2003), 95.

12 See Carl Kerényi, *Eleusis: Archetypal Image of Mother and Daughter*, trans. Ralph Manheim (Princeton: Princeton University Press, 1991), 133.

13 Kerényi, *Eleusis*, 132.

14 Gregory Nagy, 'Greek-like Elements in Linear A', *Greek, Roman, and Byzantine Studies*, 4.4 (1963): 200.

15 Maarten Jozef Vermaseren and Eugene Lane, *Cybele, Attis and Related Cults: Essays in Memory of M.J. Vermaseren* (Leiden: Brill, 1996), 370–3.

16 See Baring and Cashford, *Myth of the Goddess*.

5. Evolutionary Materialism

The cosmos is born from the woven iteration of moving matter as it spreads out. The earth and its history, including human beings, are part of this broader process that we might call 'material evolution'. This is a strange idea that sounds like a contradiction in terms. Usually, we think of matter as dead, mechanical, and passive, and we think of evolution as living, creative, and active. Lucretius, however, does not accept this duality. For Lucretius, life is an emergent property of swerving and generative material processes. The process of creation and destruction, activity and passivity, organic and inorganic, is, as Empedocles says, 'twofold'. For Lucretius, there is only nature flowing and folding itself into different patterns.

Non-living processes are just as creative and capable of novelty as living ones. This is in part because Lucretius foregrounds matter's indeterminate swerve. Accordingly, we do not find in Lucretius the same primordial crisis around the so-called 'origins of life' (the transition from matter to life) that we see in the history of modern biology and physics. Life is matter following the same basic kinetic processes of dissipation and iteration that minerals and galaxies do by other means.

Material evolution weaves together celestial, mineral, atmospheric, biological, and cultural evolution in a single process. This 'step-by-step' process is not deterministic or goal-oriented, but it does have a *directionality*. It tends towards the transformation of higher concentrations into lower ones. The movement of our cosmos 'spreads out', Lucretius says, by creating patterns and forms that increasingly dissipate motion. Kinetic forms such as spiral orbits, storm systems, watersheds, tree branches, and animal metabolisms all emerge to reduce gradients bit by bit. In transitioning from celestial to terrestrial history, Lucretius provides several stunning images highlighting their shared patterns of motion across scales. Images of vortices, dendritic veins, and woven fabrics abound in lines 5.772–925.

Commentators for generations have described Lucretius as a precursor to Darwin's theory of evolution.[1] This is true in the sense that Lucretius, in contrast to most philosophers in the ancient world, believed that living organisms emerged from nature without a predetermined design and adapted to their changing environments and one another over time. However, Lucretius was also more radical than Darwin in that he extended his theory of transmutation to the entire cosmos and human culture. The whole universe emerged from physical processes without the aid of gods, forms, or any designs given in advance. Lucretius also wholly rejected the existence of gods and their ritual worship. In contrast, Darwin was a believer and churchgoer for most of his life, only later in life claiming to be 'agnostic'.[2]

The materialist theory of emergence has had many enemies in the Western tradition. In *The Laws*, Plato wrote that those who believed that the world came into being by means other than prior design were impious and should be treated as criminals and possibly executed.[3] In the fourteenth century, Dante wrote in *The Divine Comedy* that Epicurus and his followers would spend an eternity of torture in open coffins in the sixth circle of Hell.[4]

The key argument I would like to make in this chapter is that Lucretius was not just pre-Darwinian but was also post-Darwinian in

Figure 5.1 This 1861 engraving by Gustave Doré depicts Cantos IX and X of Dante's Inferno, in which Dante and Virgil explore the Sixth Circle of Hell and speak to some of the heretics who are punished there. Here the poet listens to the account of a fellow Florentine, the Epicurean and Ghibelline leader Farinata degli Uberti. Wikimedia Commons.

his radical theory of material evolution. Lucretius' stunningly expansive theory of material evolution spans every scale of nature and culture. For Lucretius, history has only '*naturecultures*' that emerge and mix through time. History is neither deterministic nor random, but a process of indeterminate metastable emergence. I want to show this with a close reading of lines 5.772–925.

Indeterminate History

Lucretius begins this extraordinary section of Book V with a unique statement about the fundamental indeterminacy of history. Not only do all things emerge from indeterminate flows of matter, but indeterminacy does not go away. The swerve suffuses all movements of material history.

Lucretius says he has 'unraveled' [*resolvi*] (5.772) how things unfold in the blue heavens, and he is now going to 'return to the beginning of the world and the pliant [*mollia*] fields of earth' (5.780). The cosmos was woven together, and Lucretius 'unravels' it with his words to show us how. His words, though, are also woven together in metered song. So his song is a weaving that unweaves.

However, the universe is also dissipating and dying, and so unweaving him at the same time. The cosmos unweaves [*resolvi*] itself through Lucretius and his performative song. The earth then is a supple, flexible, and delicate fabric [*mollia*] woven from the cosmos (5.780–2).

> *nunc redeo ad mundi novitatem et mollia terrae*
> *arva, novo fetu quid primum in luminis oras*
> *tollere et incertis crerint committere ventis.*

> now I return to the beginning of the world and the pliant fields
> of the earth, and what first with new births they resolved
> to lift onto the shores of light and to entrust to indeterminate winds.

The '*luminis oras*' (5.781) here invokes the birth of Venus on to the shore (1.22). The indeterminate flows of wind and water swirl into turbulent metastable forms and wash up, like Venus herself, naked, on to the beach. The fabric of the flexible earth folds over itself like ocean waves. The earth and ocean lift [*tollere*] themselves from the darkness below to the light above. Once born, things are handed over [*committere*] to the world's indeterminate [*incertis*] process. The world into which life is born is one of turbulence and indeterminacy.

Figure 5.2 Salvator Rosa and studio, *Odysseus and Nausicaa* (c. 1655).
Wikimedia Commons.

From the darkness [*tenebris*] (5.777) of dissipation the world is born.
The sun dies so that we may live. Just as Odysseus washes up on shore
after being saved by Ino's woven veil, so we find ourselves in Lucretius'
Mystery initiation, washed back up on the shores of the earth. We move
into the light from the dark. The image of anabasis is manifold. Epicurus
also lifted [*tollere*] us out of the darkness and into the light (1.66–71).
However, the path upwards also has dynamic turbulence and indeterminacy that we cannot master.

Figure 5.3 Alexandre Cabanel, *The Birth of Venus* (1863). Wikimedia Commons.

This is a radical starting point for a new theory of material and biological evolution. Not only are all things emergent, but all laws and patterns are emergent as well. Emergence *itself* is an emergent property of nature, for Lucretius. Everything on earth is born by indeterminate winds, not just life. If matter is always swerving, there are no predetermined species or forms of any kind. There are no laws of biological evolution that cannot be altered by material evolution. In Lucretius' world, the earth has no plan for its creations. Life, he says, has 'free rein' in the indeterminate flux to which the earth hands it over. One organism combines with and emerges from others through something much more like symbiogenesis than Darwinian evolution.

Lucretius begins his history of life with plants because the science of bacteria did not yet exist. Earth produced, he says, 'light green plants' [*herbarum viridemque*], and then trees emerged by the contest of the plants growing into the air (5.786–7).

arboribusque datumst variis exinde per auras
crescendi magnum inmissis certamen habenis,

various trees thereafter engaged with free reins
in a great contest of growing high up into the air.

Life, for Lucretius, transforms itself by responding to its environment and other life forms. In this way, what we call genetic mutation today is only one piece of a complicated process. Plants grew large because others started growing larger. The sun also encouraged them to seek a new energy gradient. Those that can reduce a gradient faster and more efficiently live and change in response to their surroundings. The general form of plant life [*herbarum*] has no fixed essence but transforms itself in response to the world. This idea is not far from what we now call 'epigenetics' and 'environmental effects' on the organism's genetics.

Plants become what they are as emergent features of the earth. However, since the earth swerves and its airs are indeterminate, it has no plan in advance. This is not random, though, since plants' transformation is constrained by their relation to the sun and one another. Plants grow up into the turbulent air and take on its turbulence. Therefore, life has 'free rein' in a shifting set of conditions *that also have* 'free rein'.

There is a mutually constitutive 'free rein' that cannot be reduced to mere competition since competition presupposes a goal to which life's 'free rein' is struggling. The noun *certamen* seeks to capture the way trees grow as fast as possible upwards. Nature has no pregiven design or purpose, according to Lucretius. Therefore, the goal is not to survive but to experiment and try to dissipate movement – but nothing knows how best to do this in advance. So only some experiments result in survival. Evolutionary biologists often see survival as the goal simply because it was the result. However, to believe that results are goals put there in advance is to commit a 'retrospective fallacy'.

Instead, plants freely experimented with one another in the indeterminate air without a plan. They created new structures bit by bit in what we might call an 'immanent teleology'. Immanent teleology, like 'immanent causality', is a strange idea. All of nature is in entangled flux without any external cause (gods, essences, forms, laws, etc.) of its action. This is Lucretius' 'immanent materialism'. Nature could have been otherwise in another world that emerged differently than this one. Our world is not universal but singular, finite, and fleeting. It makes its path by walking. All that we can say of this world is that it will die, and its movement is one of iterative dissipation. This is the immanent indeterminacy of history (and plants).

The Tentacular Earth

Next, animals emerge. In these lines, Lucretius provides a beautiful image for the shared kinetic structure of historical development across cosmic, terrestrial, vegetal, and animal scales (5.788–92).

ut pluma atque pili primum saetaeque creantur
quadripedum membris et corpore pennipotentum,
sic nova tum tellus herbas virgultaque primum
sustulit, inde loci mortalia saecla creavit
multa modis multis varia ratione coorta,

Just as feathers, hair, and bristles are created first
on the limbs of quadrupeds and on the bodies of creatures
     powerful-of-wing,
so then the new earth offered up grass and shoots
first, and next created the races of creatures that arose
in many types by many means and in various ways.

This is such a beautiful passage because it reminds us that animals ultimately come out of the earth. In a sense, the earth is also already structured like its creatures *before* the creatures emerge. For the earth to produce animals, it must have had its own animality in a general sense. Lucretius says the earth has skin that spreads out over its surface and begins to grow up out of the surface like hair or feathers. This is not merely a projection of animality on to the earth, but an immanent expression of the earth's *animality*.

But let's slow down and consider how strange this image and its implications are. Lucretius describes the earth as a limb among many other limbs of the vast tentacular cosmos. The cosmos becomes planets when it grows limbs from its surface. The earth becomes cosmos when it grows plant limbs from its surface. Plants, therefore, are a becoming-cosmos and a becoming-earth because they are limbs with limbs. Plants are also becoming-animal as they grow limbs and fur.

In short, we have here a compelling poetic and theoretical image of the limbed [*membra*] and dendritic structure of nature. Each limb spreads out into further limbs, and so on in a vast cosmic fractal. Material history is a branching process, each limb dissipating through others. If limbs grow out of everything, then historical materialism returns to the mythopoetic images of the chthonic tentacles of the

Giants, Python, and the Minoan serpent goddess with her labyrinths and spiral meanders.

As initiates of the great Mystery, Lucretius has taken us down to the ultimate *katabasis* of the universe. Now from the darkness, the earth 'lifts' [*tollere*] (5.782) itself up into the sky. The trees 'grow up' [*crescendi*], and the creatures 'rise up' [*sustulit*] (5.791) into the shores of light [*luminis oras*], just as our planet once did from the cosmos. Humans are born as a limb with many limbs, a branch of many branches, spreading out into the cool without a fixed plan. It's a simple but profound truth that we only exist because we live in a dying universe.

Lucretius takes his description of polymorphous (5.422) animal emergence word for word from his earlier description of matter itself as '*multa modis multis primordia rerum*' (5.187). Animals emerge 'in many types by many means and in various ways' because so does matter. Morphogenesis and transmutation are not a unique feature of life but are common to all material processes. It is ultimately a consequence of matter's swerving indeterminacy that it can not only produce many *kinds* of beings but can produce them by many means. Emergence itself emerges in different ways in different worlds.

We can draw the following three conclusions about the nature of emergence in Lucretius, given the indeterminacy of the swerve.

1. There is not only one set of conditions of emergence.
2. There is not a fixed set of possible forms of life.
3. There is more than one way for forms to emerge from the same conditions.

This is also why Lucretius rejects the idea that life could have come from the sky or the oceans (5.793–4). Following Hesiod, Lucretius places chaos and indeterminacy at the heart of nature, not the male sky god (Zeus) and his ocean brother (Poseidon). Chaos, with its many tentacular limbs, gave birth to Earth (Gaia), who created out of herself without divine conception. Lucretius may also be rejecting the Platonic demiurge and the Stoic attribution of Zeus as a cosmic father.

In contrast, the earth is the immanent mother of creation, 'since from the Earth all things have been created'. Lucretius was correct that life came from the same stuff as the earth. We are children of the earth, and organic life came from inorganic processes. More than ever, it is essential not to forget this humbling naturalistic insight. We should not merely dismiss the claim that humans came out of the earth as necessarily identical to the theory of spontaneous generation, which held that life *keeps* coming out of the earth.[5] Wherever life emerged on earth, and it may have been at several different locations, it emerged from inorganic processes. Spontaneous generation theory was correct about that, but it was incorrect about the *frequency* of this occurrence.

Interestingly, Lucretius also says that creatures emerge from the earth 'of their own accord' [*sponte sua*], 'seeking sustenance and life' [*victum vitamque petentes*] (5.804). This image invokes the opening proem to Venus, whose immanent desire traverses all beings, living and non-living, and moves them into action. In Lucretius' poetic vision, life is not mechanical or passively created but is actively involved in its genesis from out of the earth. Birds, insects, and animals did not emerge fully formed from the earth, as Lucretius speculates. Nonetheless, we should take seriously the idea that, from the beginning, life was motivated by *its own desire* to live and consume energy by moving around. This is perhaps as close to a definition of life as we get in Lucretius, but even here, there is no sharp distinction between non-living and living matter.

Animals, he says, emerged from underground 'wombs' of tangled roots [*crescebant uteri terram radicibus apti*] where open veins supplied a nourishing liquid [*sucum*] that fed them (5.810–12). Animal life is pretty much the same as plant life, also 'attached to the ground by roots'. They are the same stuff as the earth and fed by the nourishing liquids of the earth (water and minerals).

The image of the earth's 'veins' [*venis*] (5.812) is another beautiful expression that traverses various scales of material order. The earth has mineral veins that turn into the 'veins' of plants, and then transform into the veins of animals. Dendritic veins traverse everything, spreading energy through all material systems like a 'wood wide web'.[6]

Lucretius continues the mythopoetic image of life coming out of the mineral-rich milky cave-wombs of Mother Earth in his description of the birth of Bacchic life (5.822–5).

terra tenet merito, quoniam genus ipsa creavit
humanum atque animal prope certo tempore fudit
omne quod in magnis bacchatur montibu' passim
aeriasque simul volucres variantibu' formis.

the name of mother deservedly, since she herself created
the human race and poured out at an almost regular rhythm
every animal that roams like Bacchus over the great
mountains, together with the birds of the air in their various forms.

Mother Earth 'poured out life in regular rhythms' [*certo tempore fudit*] (5.823), which then ran through the mountains like Bacchus. Again, we have an apt poetic image working at the mythological and naturalistic levels at the same time. Mother (Cybele) gives birth to the child (Bacchus) by pouring out like honey from the Minoan labyrinth goddess (Potnia/ Rhea). From the bowels of the dying cosmos, the goddess returns with a living son. She feeds him with regular rhythms of day and night, spring and autumn, mineral and plant juices.

At the naturalistic level, liquid life comes out of the mineral earth and pours over the land as a boundless hyper-sea.[7] From the inorganic earth comes an organic flood of free-roaming life seeking to spread out, reproduce, and mutate into various forms [*variantibu' formis*] (5.825) in the turbulent indeterminacy of the air. Life is a Bacchic shape-changing revelry. It is a 'free rein' of experimentation without plan, goal, or a single method of emergence.

Omnia Migrant

History, for Lucretius, is a profound mutagen. Time changes everything, including change itself. Nothing is fixed and solid because everything is historical. There is no Epicurean space between worlds that is outside of history. Throughout history, nature changes completely. Unlike modifications to a single substance, it is a transformation of transformation itself. Nature is not the same as itself because of history. History is the inner motor of difference inside nature (5.828–31).

> *mutat enim mundi naturam totius aetas,*
> *ex alioque alius status excipere omnia debet,*
> *nec manet ulla sui similis res: omnia migrant,*
> *omnia commutat natura et vertere cogit*

For time makes the nature of the whole world change,
and one stage has to receive everything from another,
and nothing remains similar to itself: everything migrates,
nature changes everything entirely and draws together its swerves.

There can be no higher or more important a place for history than that the one given to it by Lucretius. As nature spreads out, time passes, and the whole of nature becomes different than it was. There may be other worlds, for Lucretius, but there are also other worlds inside this world. The world is wholly other to itself. Everything is migratory not from point A to point B, but as a continual change in the whole line AB. No residue is left static, unaffected, unmoved, or outside natural history.

However, each moment in history does not come *ex nihilo* after the passing of the old nature. History is not random. Instead, each stage in nature receives, draws out, or follows the previous stage, but not deterministically. Matter is 'continually swerving' but is also related to what came before. This is the true and original meaning of the term 'dialectical and historical materialism' that Marx gets from Lucretius.[8]

Yet 'nothing remains similar to itself'. How can this be? Nature changes everything *entirely*. Nature is neither continuous nor discontinuous but is pure indeterminate flux. This is an enormous and challenging claim that goes against the entire tradition of philosophy. It is a complete rejection of all identity and substance in nature. What then is it that follows dialectically from the past if nature is wholly other to itself? What then constitutes the coherence of Ariadne's thread through the meandering labyrinth of history?

Lucretius says that nature is the 'gathering together of swerves' [*vertere cogit*] (5.831). Nature and history are gatherings of differential repetitions. They have settled rhythms of indeterminate processes. Everything that appears solid and receives its motion from another is a metastable process modulating another metastable process.

This is a critical point. History is not only dialectical but is *indeterminately dialectical* without end and with a single method or logic of emergence. This is, therefore, not at all like Hegel's dialectics of contradiction and synthesis. There can be no contradiction for Lucretius because nature never produces an identity that could have an opposite. There is no raising up of nature into a higher unity, *but the inverse*. There is only *katabasis* or ongoing iterative dissipation tending towards maximum entropy in the heat-death of the universe. It is, strictly speaking, Hegel's worst nightmare.

However, the process of death and dissipation, for Lucretius, is not merely negative. The process of decay is simultaneously creative and generative, to a point. This is the profound truth for those who had drunk the *kykeon* at Eleusis. Persephone dies in one season and is reborn

Figure 5.4 Frederic, Lord Leighton, *The Return of Persephone* (1891). Wikimedia Commons.

in another. There is no reason to fear death, it is not a lack. It is a creative transformation undergone by the world (5.832–6).

namque aliud putrescit et aevo debile languet,
porro aliud concrescit et e contemptibus exit,

sic igitur mundi naturam totius aetas
mutat, et ex alio terram status excipit alter,
quod tulit ut nequeat, possit quod non tulit ante.

For one thing rots and weakens enfeebled with age,
and then another grows up and emerges from scorned beginnings.
So therefore time makes the nature of the whole world
change, and one stage receives the earth from another,
so that what bore cannot, and what did not bear before, can.

Python's dead body rots underground, but from her fumes she creates
a material knowledge of the cosmos. The truth and beauty of the material world are that novelty comes from 'putrescence' [*putrescit*] (5.833)
and the 'abject' [*contemptibus*] (5.834). Death, decomposition, and putrescence make the whole world change and bar any static identity, forms,
and gods. The only god is the dying goddess of matter.

Lucretius gives us a beautiful poetic image of this dialectical process.
History proceeds step by step, receiving and iterating what came before
in a novel way. However, it is precisely the *giving unto death* that lets the
next movement be creative in a way that it could not previously, since it
had not yet moved through the indeterminacy of death.

Monstrous Matters

The earth is a monster, or rather a monster of monsters. According to
Lucretius, she creates immanently, like Venus, the goddess of desire and
swerving inclination, from herself out of herself without any prior design
or end. She is pure 'abundance' (5.870) and excess. When matter creates
without forms or a craftsman, it 'produces wondrous contrasting revela-
tions' [*portenta creare conatast mira*] (5.837).

The Latin world *monstra*, from which the English word 'monster' comes,
is 'a wonder, prodigy, or marvel'. The earth creates amazing 'portents'
[*portenta*] that express its range of experimentation and creation, which
has nothing to do with reproduction. Nature does not direct itself towards
sexual reproduction or the creation of species *directly*. It creates asexually,
non-sexually, and 'runs all sorts of things together' [*rebus concurrere*].[9] The
origin of species, therefore, does not resemble species at all. This is a
deeply Darwinian insight as well. Species are metastable emergent entities. The monster is the opposite of a sexually reproducing species.

In other words, the process that produces species is not one of identical forms but of divergent differences that create both species and monsters together without preference or aim. It is much more like a 'symbiogenesis', where organisms live together to produce a larger body.[10] According to Hesiod, Gaia loved all her wondrous/monstrous children, who acted as portents or signs of her experimental creativity. They were portents of the 'free rein' of the swerve. This divine earthly love of hybrid creatures and monsters was also part of the extensive Minoan depiction of sacred hybrid creatures such as the Minotaur. Monsters were not feared or evil but had a prodigal knowledge of nature as a process of *swerving hybridisation*. They were wonders or miracles evidencing the novelty of nature.

The hatred and exile of monstrous hybrids does not begin, according to Hesiod, until the sky god Ouranos arrives and creates, with Gaia, the Titans, the Hekatonkheires (one-hundred-handed giants), and the Cyclopes (one-eyed giants). Ouranos despised them and locked them up in the underworld (Tartarus). Later, the Olympians hated the monsters and tried to slay them in the Titanomachy and the Gigantomachy. Lucretius thus invokes this earliest pre-Greek mythic tradition in which the underworld of monsters was a site of hybridisation, putrefaction, creativity, and not of 'evil'.

We can see in the persecution of monsters the philosophical privileging of form over matter. Matter creates monsters that do not con*form* to hetero-reproductive models of species, essence, or rational forms. The narrative of monsters as evil 'de*form*ations' and aberrations from 'normal' approved forms is an insidious way that history has tried to ignore the creativity of matter and nature. To admit that matter can make new forms would be to acknowledge the derivative and monstrous nature of all forms. So monstrous matter must always be 'a freak'. Lucretius, Hesiod, and the Minoans remind us, though, that the earth made and loved all its monsters.

This is not only an issue in mythology. Contemporary biology is finally coming round to acknowledging the critical role of trans-species couplings and symbiogenesis.[11] Nature produces real bacterial and viral monsters. We should take Lucretius' general point here seriously. Nature creates creatures with all kinds of limbs, mixed genders, and morphologies that do not allow them to reproduce (5.835–50). However, Lucretius does not say that this is a deficiency, failure, or an abomination. Instead, nature's 'queer' ecology (from the Latin word *torqueō*, meaning to twist, whirl, or swerve) is not aimed at the reproduction of heterosexual forms but is pure morphogenesis. Lucretius mentions that 'many races of animals must have died out' (5.855) in this way, but this is not an ethical judgement. Species do not last forever, for Lucretius. The difference between monsters and species then is not ontological but temporal. Some forms stick around longer than others.

We see some creatures survive by 'feeding on the life-giving breezes' due to their craftiness, speed, courage, or defences (5.857–67). Others survive by living with humans and making themselves as useful to humans as humans are to them (5.870–7). Lucretius stresses that domestication was a mutual and voluntary act that particular animals 'desired' [*cupide*] (5.868) 'of their own volition' [*sponte sua*] (5.872). This is an intriguing theory of co-evolution in which species survive not only because of the natural wild environment but also because of their ability to adapt to other animal cultures, in this case, human civilisation. Human evolution occurred only with domestic animals and vice versa. The two create an interspecies assemblage or 'companion species'.[12]

Nature is experimental, swerving, queer, and creative, but that does not mean that *anything* is possible. If anything were possible, nature would be random, but this is not the case. History proceeds step by step, iterating itself *relationally*, not *randomly*. Therefore, 'although many seeds of things existed in the earth' [*in terris semina rerum*], many things 'are not able to be woven into existence together, but each thing proceeds in its own manner, and all by a settled rhythm of nature safeguard their individual differences' [*non tamen inter se possunt complexa creari, sed res quaeque suo ritu procedit, et omnes foedere naturae certo discrimina servant*] (5.922–4).

Many different types of seeds mix and weave together, but once particular metastable formations mix, not all animals or limbs can weave together. Settled emergent patterns of natural processes defend and protect the singularity of things such that things are neither equal nor randomly related. Randomness assumes equality of relation. However, the *foedere naturae* settles into patterns [*ritu*] and habits [*solerent*] that make each process 'run together' [*concurrere*] and 'weave together' [*complexa*] in a singular way.

This is an important lesson about nature. Nature is not looking to produce perfection. It is swerving, deviant, experimental, and it tends to *increase* and multiply differences. Nature is a difference multiplier. Everything, Lucretius says, has its own 'interval' [*discrimina*] and 'settled rhythm' [*certo tempore*]. Therefore, there may be diverse and wondrous animals, but there are no Centaurs and no Scyllas. Instead of rejecting mythology outright as Plato, Pindar, Xenophanes, and others did, however, Lucretius invokes the more profound truth of mythology without adopting it literally.

Conclusion

Material evolution is neither deterministic nor random but experimental, improvisational, and indeterministic. Nature, in general, and the earth, in particular, have no plan in advance but proceed step by step, just as Lucretius does in his poem. Life, for Lucretius, does not come from the gods but directly from non-living matter. Evolution has no goal but proceeds by running together the swerving of nature into metastable patterns, which may or may not reproduce themselves as species.

In this chapter, I looked closely at lines 5.772–925 in which Lucretius describes the metastable emergence of plant and animal life. In the next lines of the poem, Lucretius offers several compelling theories of human life, culture, language, art, politics, and religion. In the next chapter, I look at Lucretius' highly original cultural history of humanity.

Notes

1   'Lucretius was seen as an ally of Darwin as soon as *Origin of Species* was published, and although DRN's importance as an anti-Creationist text then faded somewhat, eclipsed by Darwin, it was still seen as a precursor of Darwinism.' Gordon Campbell, *Lucretius on Creation and Evolution: A Commentary on De Rerum Natura 5.772–1104* (Oxford: Oxford University Press, 2003), 6. For the reception of Lucretius in the eighteenth and nineteenth centuries, see George D. Hadzsits, *Lucretius and His Influence* (New York: Cooper Square Publishers, 1963), 317–32; and W. R. Johnson, *Lucretius and the Modern World* (London: Duckworth, 2000), 103ff. See Campbell, *Lucretius on Creation and Evolution*, 6: 'This has remained the position ever since, and many textbooks on evolution that include a history of the development of evolutionary theories describe Lucretius, along with Empedocles, as an ancient Evolutionist, or make general references to "Greek thinkers" as Daniel Dennett does.' Campbell references Daniel Dennett, *Darwin's Dangerous Idea: Evolution and the Meanings of Life* (New York: Touchstone, 1995), 17ff.
2   Momme von Sydow, 'Charles Darwin: A Christian Undermining Christianity?', in David M. Knight and Matthew D. Eddy (eds),

Science and Beliefs: From Natural Philosophy to Natural Science, 1700–1900 (Burlington, VT: Ashgate, 2005), 141–56.

3 Plato, *The Laws* (London: Penguin, 1970), 415–20.

4 Dante, *The Inferno* (New York: Signet, 1982), 96.

5 See Lucretius, *De Rerum Natura*, 5.795–800. As Blundell says: 'By the late fifth century the theory was firmly established that the first human beings were born from the ground, that earth and water were the substances of which they were composed, and that heat was an agent in their manufacture . . . No other basic hypothesis, so far as we know, was ever put forward in scientific philosophy.' Sue Blundell, *The Origins of Civilization in Greek and Roman Thought* (London: Croom Helm, 1986), 48.

6 Merlin Sheldrake, *Entangled Nature* (London: Random House, 2020).

7 Mark McMenamin and Dianna McMenamin, *Hypersea: Life on Land* (New York: Columbia University Press, 1996).

8 See Thomas Nail, *Marx in Motion: A New Materialist Marxism* (Oxford: Oxford University Press, 2020), ch. 1.

9 Catriona Mortimer-Sandilands and Bruce Erickson (eds), *Queer Ecologies: Sex, Nature, Politics, Desire* (Bloomington: Indiana University Press, 2010).

10 Lynn Margulis and Dorion Sagan, *Microcosmos: Four Billion Years of Microbial Evolution* (Berkeley: University of California Press, 1986).

11 Margulis and Sagan, *Microcosmos*.

12 Donna Haraway, *The Companion Species Manifesto: Dogs, People, and Significant Otherness* (Chicago: Prickly Paradigm Press, 2003).

6. A Brief History of Language

Book V is the longest in the whole of *De Rerum Natura*. In particular, the last six hundred lines of the poem compose an epic of human history within the greater epic of nature that the book describes. In these short lines, Lucretius covers all of human history leading up to his present day. He begins Book V with cosmic emergence, then moves on to the workings of our immediate solar system, then to terrestrial emergence, concluding with a brief history of human civilisation. The kinetic patterns of flows, vortices, and dendrites traverse all scales.

Human history is deeply intertwined in cosmic history for Lucretius, even though we tend to think of our inventions as unique and distinct from nature. Human culture is part of the material evolution of our dissipating universe. Culture is wholly material and natural, just as nature is cultural. There is no ontological division between cosmic and terrestrial scales, but only differences of degree and organisation of the same basic material processes of dissipation, iteration, and transformation.

This chapter aims to look closely at lines 5.925–1101 and to spell out Lucretius' most novel theoretical moves regarding human history and the origins of language, which continue to challenge philosophy and history today. In particular, my argument in this chapter is that Lucretius shows us that human history follows the same material patterns or 'settled rhythms' [*certo tempore*] as the rest of natural history.

Wild Strawberries

Human beings come from the earth. Lucretius does not say precisely how humans emerged but only, quite accurately, that they were 'hardier' [*durius*] with more 'solid bones' [*solidis magis ossibus*] (5.925–6). Palaeolithic humans did have more substantial and robust bone structures than modern humans. This was due to, among other things, their relatively greater mobility compared with sedentary agricultural and modern humans.[1] Lucretius highlights this increased mobility when he sings (5.931–2).

multaque per caelum solis volventia lustra
volgivago vitam tractabant more ferarum,

During many revolutions of the sun orbiting through the sky
they passed their lives in the Bacchic and roaming manner of wild beasts.

Humans wandered about everywhere, roved, and rambled as inconstant vagrants [*volgivago*] (5.932). In this way, they were like the wild animals who travel like Bacchus through the mountains [*bacchatur montibu' passim*] (5.824). Of all the things to say about the first human beings, it is fascinating that movement should be a prominent feature for Lucretius. Movement and mobility are critical aspects of human history, anatomy, and culture. When humans are not permitted free movement or are not engaged in active lifestyles of some kind, there are negative social and physiological consequences. Wandering also provides a beautiful poetic image common across scales of nature. Lucretius says that celestial bodies roam like sheep, animals roam like Bacchus, humans roam like the beasts [*ferarum*], and everything wanders the cosmos as swerving matter [*omnia migrant*] (5.830).

Early humans did not know how to till the earth and plant seeds. They took everything the earth 'created of its own volition' [*terra crearat sponte sua*] as a 'gift' [*donum*], and it 'pleased their hearts well enough' (5.939). Significantly, Lucretius uses the poetic phrase '*sponte sua*' seven times throughout Book V to indicate the 'spontaneous agency' of the earth, insects, animals, and nature more broadly. Faithful to his theoretical starting point, Lucretius treats matter as active and creative through history as well. This blurs the lines between nature, which we typically think of as passive, and culture, which we think of as active. For Lucretius, there are only '*naturecultures*'.[2]

Nature is not merely a passive object *of* history or 'useful stuff' to be instrumentalised by the 'real' cultural agents of history. Nature is a spontaneous, excessive, and generous 'gift' that early humans treated as such. Their relationship to the earth was one of reciprocity and mutual gifting. The earth gave them life, and they gave it back when the time came. 'They cared for their bodies amidst acorn-bearing oaks' and ate 'wild strawberries' when they grew (5.940–2).

Lucretius' vision of the earliest humans is not a simple progress story, nor is it a romantic vision of noble savages. Early humans went hungry, and wild animals attacked them. However, their bodies were also more durable. Wild nature grew more and larger wild berries. One of the most significant effects of agriculture is that it destroyed many wild plants and animals and depleted the soil of nutrients, such that wild foods were less plentiful.[3]

This is not a simple story of a 'golden age', yet we must admit that Lucretius was right about the supply of wild strawberries. Instead of forcing the earth to yield a few kinds of grain, early humans ate a much wider variety of whatever nature gifted them. It was a very different kind of relationship that we will return to in a later and stunning passage.

Lucretius describes the earth's novelty as a flower [*novitas tum florida mundi*], unfolding out of itself [*sponte sua*] gradually, step by step. Humans were 'poor' [*miseris*], while at the same time supplied with ample food of all kinds from this flowering novelty (5.943–4). For Lucretius, the earth has agency, since its running rivers and springs actively called out to the humans [*fluvii fontesque vocabant*] to slake their thirst. Water rushes down from the mountains and 'loudly summons them from afar' [*claricitat late sitientia*]. The first speech on earth, according to Lucretius, is, therefore, the speech of the earth itself. In particular, it is the *vocabant* of the flowing streams that spoke to and taught humans to speak and listen to the earth. It was their first experience of something like the numinous.

It is no coincidence then that, following the water's summons, humans inhabited the sylvan temples of the nymphs where the 'bubbling and gushing' [*scatere atque erumpere*] of water gathered them together to drink but also to speak and listen to one another and to nature (5.948–52).

denique nota vagis silvestria templa tenebant
nympharum, quibus e scibant umori' fluenta
lubrica proluvie larga lavere umida saxa,
umida saxa, super viridi stillantia musco,
et partim plano scatere atque erumpere campo.

In addition they inhabited sylvan temples of the nymphs, discovered on their wanderings, from which they knew flowing streams of water washed over the wet rocks with a great flood –
the wet rocks – dripping over the green moss from above,
and bubbling and gushing here and there on the level plain.

This is a crucial feature of the material origins of language, natural religion, and human society. Lucretius suggests that natural springs of fresh water under shaded groves were the site and source of the first human gatherings. The great twentieth-century historian Lewis Mumford argued the same thing.[4] In these sheltered grottos, humans were not only called to freshwater sources but, as Lucretius suggests, something more profound and numinous. Humans likely returned seasonally to these unique places and found one another with more frequency. The springs offered nourishment, and the groves protected them from the view of predators. Humans were also calmed, lulled, or settled [*sedare*] by the waters (5.945).

The sound of babbling water is calming, and perhaps, as Lucretius' images suggest, these sacred pools of water contained a visual knowledge that humans understood intuitively. Water mainly flows and wanders [*vagis*] over the land, but at certain unique places it pools, calms, and settles down. Perhaps humans learned to settle from watching the water. After watching water move endlessly over the earth, they finally encountered the direct source of its flowing at the spring. The image of the spring or fount regularly invoked throughout Lucretius' poem[5] is an image of ongoing creativity, flow, and natural generosity. Even in winter, many springs continue to flow and thus express a kind cosmic knowledge or significance about the unlimited nature of things. Nature moves, dissipates, iterates, and transforms. Nature, like water, is a shape-changer.

The sacred grove and the tree of wisdom frequently appear in Minoan art and religious icons. As Paul Valéry says in his 'Dialogue of the Tree' (1943) in the persona of Lucretius, the tree is also a fountain, spreading out and up, dissipating water from the ground to the sky, and iterating itself with every fractal dendrite of its being.[6] The tree is a material image of a dissipating cosmos.

For Lucretius, the spring grove is the first temple because it speaks, through its bubbling and babbling, the truth of the cosmos: that everything flows. The bubbles of the spring invoke Venus, the goddess of bubbles and foam to whom *De Rerum Natura* is dedicated. The image of pure and clean water is, as the French philosopher Gaston Bachelard writes, a poetic image of knowledge and transparency.

The whole scene tells us everything that is most important to know about nature. The trees change and iterate with the seasons, speaking with their leaves in the wind. Meanwhile, the spring overflows generously underneath. It is no coincidence that the two oldest and most

Figure 6.1 Ruins of the Temple of Zeus in Dodona. Wikimedia Commons.

respected oracles in ancient Greece expressed these twin aspects of the original sacred grotto. The first is the pre-Greek temple at Dodona. We know little about its pre-Greek origins, but the oracle was an ancient oak tree that spoke through the wind in its branches.[7] The second is the legendary oracle of Delphi, which began as a pre-Greek oracular spring governed by the nymph-priestess Telphusa until it was taken over by Apollo and Dionysus.[8]

Opposed to *religio*, which binds by law, the *templa nympharum* has a material knowledge that is inseparable from what it does, namely to *flow*. The grove does not proceed by binding but by 'running together' [*concurrere*] the wandering [*vagis*] flows of humans, animals, plants, and water, gathering them up in a pool or puddle without closing anything off from anything else. The sacred grove is the original free association of humans with one another and with nature. It is a place to talk, listen, and learn about the nature of things, their source, and death. It is a place of notable [*nota*] gradient reduction where nutrients move rapidly from more to less concentrated areas as they spread out.

We may never know the origins of the first human gatherings and their first feelings of the numinous. However, there is good historical

Figure 6.2 John William Waterhouse, *A Naiad or Hylas with a Nymph* (1893). Wikimedia Commons.

reason to believe that Lucretius' image of the *templa nympharum* is a possible and probable one. Some of the first sacred places were likely wooded grottos and springs for reasons not reducible to their utility.

Lucretius says that these early wild strawberry eating humans did not know how to use fire or wear clothing or make houses. They did not have laws. They only took what fortune [*fortuna*] carried to them and used it spontaneously [*sponte sua*] as they had received it. They lived with a high degree of natural indeterminacy. This was not a utopia by any means but rather the free play of Venus and Mars with highly turbulent and mixed outcomes. 'Venus brought together the bodies of lovers in the forests' either by mutual longing, violence, or gifts of 'acorns and wild strawberries or choice pears'. For Lucretius, the first human economies were ones of unequal and asymmetrical exchange. Before there was any notion of unity, identity, and equality, there was only gift and theft. Economic utility and exchange were not essential features of human nature or gifts from the gods.

Lucretius, consistent with Book IV, thus also acknowledges the existence of female sexual desire. However, he also notes the danger of male sexual violence. This is hardly a romantic ideal, but neither is it an entirely pessimistic history that is fully resolved by later social 'progress'. The earliest humans lived in rhythm with light and dark alternation, love and death, without fearing that otherworldly gods would punish them or that the sun would not come up again (5.972–6). They also, however, feared wild animal attacks and were 'ripped by their teeth' until 'savagely intense pain took away their life' (5.990–6). The primal world of human history included its share of asymmetrical violence, but it is not as though civilisation abolished death and violence. If anything, according to Lucretius, murder and rape become institutionalised and systemic with the rise of civilisation.

At least for early humans, Lucretius says, 'one day did not consign many thousands of men on active duty to their destruction' in war, or one storm kill many boatloads of men at a time. Early human societies sometimes starved from lack of food, but in modern ones, 'overabundance drowns them'. 'Once people often used to pour poison for themselves unwittingly, now they give it to others more cleverly' (5.1006–9). Early humans had a simple abundance, but the modern quest for 'more' also encouraged the 'immoderate and restless [*improba*] art of sailing' and colonial violence that willingly killed so many unnecessarily. Lucretius is unequivocal on this point: 'the greater fault belongs, I think, to us' (5.1425). At least early humans died in the struggle for survival, Lucretius says, whereas modern societies intentionally die and murder for wealth, religion, and power.

The past was not wholly good or bad, nor is the present. Historical method gives us a perspective to learn from our experiments without the burden of the gods or arbitrary notions of progress based on a fetishisation of the present. Lucretius seeks to liberate history from all the narratives of progress and reclaim it as an experimental process or mixture of techniques that can be used or left behind. History is, therefore, also a deeply ethical practice for Lucretius, as we will discuss shortly.

Once humans had 'huts, pelts, and fire, and women, joined to men, agreed into one', and 'they saw offspring born from themselves, then the human race first began to soften' (5.1011–14). As humans increasingly settled with more and more people, a significant transition occurred: the invention of language and society.

A Materialist Theory of Language

The human use of fire had enormous historical implications. It increased the length of the 'day' and allowed human activity to go on for longer at night. Large hearths made possible long periods of night-time social gatherings around the fire, leading to increased social interactions.

Several recent theorists suggest, as Lucretius did, that these fires were significant in the development of language.[9]

Lucretius adds that these fires also had critical physiological consequences for the human body, which no longer needed to be as tough-skinned. Night-time social interactions led to increased bonding, which reduced the acceptability of male domination and sexual violence [*inminuit viris*] (5.1015–17).

ignis enim curavit ut alsia corpora frigus
non ita iam possent caeli sub tegmine ferre,
et Venus inminuit viris

For fire ensured that their shivering bodies were not so
able to endure cold beneath the cover of the sky,
and Venus lessened their male centeredness,

After the invention of fire, the acts of Venus became increasingly important, and humans multiplied. Accordingly, the first human figurative sculptures were what we call 'Venus' figurines depicting women with enlarged buttocks, bellies, and breasts, displaying fertility. Raising children with a social group further 'broke down the harsh characters of the parents' (5.1019–26).

tunc et amicitiem coeperunt iungere aventes
finitimi inter se nec laedere nec violari,
et pueros commendarunt muliebreque saeclum,
vocibus et gestu cum balbe significarent
imbecillorum esse aequum misererier omnis,
nec tamen omnimodis poterat concordia gigni,
sed bona magnaque pars servabat foedera caste
aut genus humanum iam tum foret omne peremptum,
nec potuisset adhuc perducere saecla propago.

Then too neighbors began to form friendships
among themselves desiring neither to injure or be harmed,
and sought out protection for children and the race of women,
and making it known by voices and gestures in stuttering speech
that it was right for everyone to take pity on the weak.
Nor nevertheless was harmony entirely able to be produced,
but a good part, the majority, kept the agreements faithfully,
or the human race even then would have all perished,

Children made their parents less haughty, proud, vain, arrogant, and domineering [*superbus*]. Fire, increased sex, children, friendships, and human languages co-emerged together to shape early human culture.

The rivers and babbling springs called [*vocabant*] (5.945) to humans, then humans called [*vocibus*] to one another with gestures, movements, actions [*gestu*], and stuttering [*balbe*]. These gestures formed an experimental performance without the support of any prior system of agreed-upon coordination. The structure of language, according to Lucretius, was not built into humans (the innate theory). Nor did language emerge suddenly out of nowhere (the discontinuity theory). Instead, it was a mixture of natural sounds and motions learned from the natural movements and sounds of rivers, animals, the wind through the trees in the sacred grove (the continuity theory), plus the social coordination of human sounds to natural sounds (social interaction theory).

Language, for Lucretius, is continuous with the natural world of sound and the social world. These are, after all, not separate realms. Language comes from a naturally speaking world and social egalitarianism. From the beginning, according to Lucretius, human language practices emerged to ensure the equal sharing of life's hardships among all [*aequum misererier omnis*] (5.1023). Therefore, human language developed in a partnership model with other humans and nature and was deeply political. It aimed at social peace.

However, Lucretius is also explicit that language did not guarantee perfect harmony [*concordia*]. Language does not mean everyone agrees or that communication necessarily achieves peace. *Discordia* is just as much a part of society as it is of human minds and nature. If nature is fundamentally turbulent and humans are part of nature, then human bodies, minds, and cultures are turbulent. Human society did not emerge as a war of each against all, nor did it begin with perfect noble savages. It appeared as a way to try and collectively weather the indeterminacy of nature and social life without trying to dominate or control everything. As long as most people 'protected the agreement faithfully' [*servabat foedera caste*] (5.1024), then human beings could survive together.

Language then, for Lucretius, was not merely an arbitrary system of communication. It was an immanent condition of material co-evolution and society. Without it, humans would not have formed social groups. Humans used naturally occurring sounds and gestures, just as they used plants and minerals to help them establish rhythms with the world. This does not mean that the *purpose* of language was survival, but that first and foremost, it was an expression of the nature of things to dissipate iteratively. It was a process of sound that was continued by other means through humans. Language is not a system of ideal abstractions or representations. It is a material process continuous with the rest of nature.

As a physical activity, language helps humans dissipate more energy by iterating coordinated movements and sounds. The invention of human language is yet another way for the material evolution of nature to seek out and break down new gradients. For instance, instead of going to sleep, humans sat around the fire and found new techniques to expend more energy: language, politics, sex, and storytelling.

Lucretius also makes the interesting claim that the first human language was visual and gestural. Only later did it become auditory. It was nature that drove and pushed [*subegit*] the human tongue to start making different sounds in addition to gestures (5.1028–33).

At varios linguae sonitus natura subegit
mittere, et utilitas expressit nomina rerum,
non alia longe ratione atque ipsa videtur
protrahere ad gestum pueros infantia linguae,
cum facit ut digito quae sint praesentia monstrent,

But nature forced them to utter the different sounds
of the tongue, and practical advantage fashioned the names of things,
in a way not far different than the tongue's very
lack of speech leads children to employ gestures,
when it makes them point with a finger at things that are present.

Just as matter swerves, so does the tongue. Human language, for Lucretius, is a material emergence like the horns that erupt from a calf's forehead (5.1033–4), or the claws that come out of baby tiger paws (5.1036), or the 'shaky' wings of baby birds (5.1040). This is a fascinating poetic image. Lucretius likens the tongue to a physiological appendage inside the mouth. Each creature finds a way to move its appendages to speak. Gesture and visual languages come first. Then, once there are tongues, the tongue becomes just another limb to make sonic gestures.

Humans can move their tongues to make various noises. In the most general sense, language is the gesticulation of limbs, including those spread out by the whole universe. If language is first and foremost gestural and kinetic, then to some degree everything that moves is communicating something, in this general sense. This is an unorthodox idea, but its implications for thinking about natural language and culture could be vast.

De Rerum Nominibus

Where did humans get the names of things? For Lucretius, the idea that 'one individual then distributed names to things and that humans learned the first words from him is absurd' (5.1041–2). If one person can move their tongue to make noise, so could others. Material language began as a collective egalitarian process of 'conjoining marked utterances' [cuncta notare vocibus] (5.1043–4). Language coordinates one movement with another such that when the first appears, one expects a second to follow. However, over time, humans began to think that the first motion 'represented' the second and that the second was like the ideal, immaterial essence of the first.[10] Again, historical materialism can help show us the true nature of things that have been forgotten and covered over by idealism.

The Latin word notare (to mark) also suggests that there is no ontological division between gesture, speech, and writing. Movements always occur alongside other movements. So, when we coordinate movements [cuncta], gesture, speech, and writing occur together simultaneously. Sounds, for example, physically mark and inscribe the world as simulacra (sound waves) diffract with one another and bounce off things.

Lucretius wholly rejects idealist theories of language in which meaning derives from the minds of humans. Human language, for the poet, is the continuation of natural language by other means. Language first occurs in the world. Later it is expressed in the bodies and minds of human groups. Then eventually, much later, individuals conceptualise it as a coherent system.

'If others too had not used their voices with one another, from where was the notion of utility implanted and from where was this power first granted to him, to know what he wanted to do and conceive it in his mind' (5.1046–9)? There is no progress in language or history, for Lucretius, only collective experimentations that respond to and play off one another. Language may be useful, but use itself is an emergent and changing feature of history. Language and history do not originate in the minds of great men but through the practical experiments of naturalcultural collectives. This also means that language and history are not closed or completed systems. They are open like the universe itself to flow and spread out creatively, as in a relay.

Human language and the names of things do not emerge out of nowhere, *ex nihilo*. Before humans, other animals were already 'accustomed to let out different and various voices [*dissimilis soleant voces variasque*] when fear or pain is present, and then when they burst with joy' (5.1059–61). Well before Darwin's famous description of animal emotions in *The Expression of the Emotions in Man and Animals* (1872), Lucretius had already given several detailed empirical examples of animal emotion and communication. Dogs show their teeth and growl when angered, gently nip at their puppies, howl when lonely, and initiate play by lowering their bodies and dodging blows. A horse's whinnying is different when spurred by winged Venus and when snorting for a skirmish (5.1073–6). Birds, too, have 'different and various voices' that 'indicate

Figure 6.3 Charles Darwin, *The Expression of the Emotions in Man and Animals* (1872), fig. 14, 'Head of snarling Dog. From life, by Mr. Wood.' Author's signature is at bottom left. Wikimedia Commons.

different things with one sound or another' (5.1090). Some noises are for hunting, some for fighting, and others depend on the weather. The more we have studied animal sounds, following Lucretius' observations, the more we have discovered animal languages.[11]

For Lucretius, human language did not emerge *in contrast* to animal language but as a continuation of it. It would be 'absolutely amazing', according to Lucretius, if humans, as animals, were *not* able to use their tongues to make various noises like other animals (5.1056). Therefore, humans merely continue in their own way what nature already does in a more general sense. For example, Lucretius says that fire was not given to humans by gods but rather by natural lightning strikes. Humans watched natural fires cook plants and animals, then used fire to do the same (5.1094–101). In this early phase of human history, humans learned from and continued natural habits and patterns in various ways. They did so in relative equality and abundance, but certainly not in perfect harmony or total safety. They lived with a degree of indeterminacy and turbulence in nature that they knew they could not master.

Conclusion

However, as civilisation expanded, humans tried to overcome and secure their fate against the swerving of nature using states, walls, laws, religion, and warfare – all to disastrous effect, according to Lucretius, as we will see in the next chapter.

Notes

1   Christopher B. Ruff, Brigitte Holt, Markku Niskanen, Vladmir Sladek, Margit Berner, Evan Garofalo, Heather M. Garvin, Martin Hora, Juho-Antti Junno, Eliska Schuplerova, Rosa Vilkama, and Erin Whittey, 'Gradual Decline in Mobility with the Adoption of Food Production in Europe', *Proceedings of the National Academy of Sciences of the United States of America (PNAS)*, 112.23 (2015): 7147–52, https://www. pnas.org/content/112/23/7147 (accessed 12 July 2021).

2   See Vicki Kirby (ed.), *What If Culture Was Nature All Along?* (Edinburgh: University of Edinburgh Press, 2017).

3   James Scott, *Against the Grain: A Deep History of the Earliest States* (New Haven: Yale University Press, 2017).

4   'In going back so far for the origins of the city, one must not of course

overlook the practical needs that drew family groups and tribes together seasonally in a common habitat, a series of camp sites, even in a collecting or a hunting economy. These played their parts, too; and long before agricultural villages and towns became a feature of the neolithic culture, the favorable sites for them had probably been prospected: the pure spring with its year-round supply of water, the solid hummock of land, accessible, yet protected by river or swamp, the nearby estuary heavily stocked with fish and shellfish – all these served already in many regions for the intermediary mesolithic economy, on sites whose permanence is witnessed by huge mounds of opened shells [. . .] In the earliest gathering about a grave or a painted symbol, a great stone or a sacred grove, one has the beginning of a succession of civic institutions that range from the temple to the astronomical observatory, from the theater to the university. Thus even before the city is a place of fixed residence, it begins as a meeting place to which people periodically return: the magnet comes before the container, and this ability to attract non-residents to it [. . .] The first germ of the city, then, is in the ceremonial meeting place that serves as the goal for pilgrimage: a site to which family or clan groups are drawn back, at seasonable intervals, because it concentrates, in addition to any natural advantages it may have, certain "spiritual" or supernatural powers, powers of higher potency and greater duration, of wider cosmic significance, than the ordinary processes of life. And though the human performances may be occasional and temporary, the structure that supports it, whether a paleolithic grotto or a Mayan ceremonial center with its lofty pyramid, will be endowed with a more lasting cosmic image.' Lewis Mumford, *The City in History: Its Origins, its Transformations, and its Prospects* (San Diego: Harcourt, 1961), 9–10.

5   See Michel Serres, *The Birth of Physics*, trans. David Webb and William Ross, 2nd edn (Lanham, MD: Rowman and Littlefield International, 2018).

6   Paul Valéry, 'Dialogue of the Tree', in *Collected Works of Paul Valéry, Vol. 4: Dialogues*, trans. William M. Stewart (Princeton: Princeton University Press, 1956), 153–76.

7   Jessica Piccinini, *The Shrine of Dodona in the Archaic and Classical Ages: A History* (Macerata: EUM-Edizioni Università di Macerata, 2017).

8   'Hymn to Apollo', in *The Homeric Hymns*, trans. Susan C. Shelmerdine (Newburyport, MA: Focus/R. Pullins, 1995), 62–90. See also Joseph Fontenrose, 'The Spring Telphusa', *Transactions and Proceedings of the American Philological Association*, 100 (1969): 119–31.

9   See R. I. M. Dunbar, Clive Gamble, and J. A. J. Gowlett (eds), *Lucy to Language: The Benchmark Papers* (Oxford: Oxford University Press, 2014); and J. A. J. Gowlett, 'The Discovery of Fire by Humans: a Long and Convoluted Process', *Phil. Trans. R. Soc. B*, 371 (2016): 20150164.

10   See Thomas Nail, *Being and Motion* (Oxford: Oxford University Press, 2019), ch. 15.

11   See C. N. Slobodchikoff, Bianca S. Perla, and Jennifer L. Verdolin, *Prairie Dogs: Communication and Community in an Animal Society* (Cambridge, MA: Harvard University Press, 2009); and Jason Daley, 'Researchers Translate "Bat Talk". Turns Out They Argue – A Lot', *Smithsonian Magazine*, 23 December 2016, https://www.smithsonianmag.com/smart-news/researchers-translate-bat-talk-and-they-argue-lot-180961564/ (accessed 12 July 2021).

7. Eros and Civilisation

Civilisation is the systematic attempt to divide, hierarchise, and control the vast turbulent movements of nature. It is one response to the flow of history towards dissipation. Instead of floating downstream like the ones who ate wild strawberries around the sacred grove, civilisation declares war on nature. It invents kings, laws, war, and religion. Unlike language, the arts, weaving, planting, and metallurgy, humans did not learn about imperialism and religion directly from nature. At some point, humans decided to sail upstream against the entropic current of history.

They saw themselves as something different from, and even contrary to, nature. As the French philosopher Michel Serres summarises this position,

> Man is a stranger to the world, to the dawn, to the sky, to things. He hates them and struggles against them. His environment is a dangerous enemy to be fought and kept in servitude. Martial neuroses, from Plato to Descartes, from Bacon to our time. The hatred of objects at the root of knowledge, the horror of the world at the foundation of theory.[1]

The harder civilisation struggles to slow the erosion and dissipation of the world around it, according to Lucretius, the more it hastens its demise.

When all looks bleak for humans in their losing battle against nature, Lucretius finds solace and hope in the history of art, pleasure, and wisdom at the end of Book V. In only a handful of short lines, Lucretius paints one of the most beautiful and revealing images of the good life or what we might call his 'aesthetic communism'. Nature teaches humans how to make art, and like a relay, they pick it up and begin to experiment with it step by step. Instead of moving against the flow of history and nature, they take refuge in the performative act of iterative dissipation (eating, singing, dancing, and making art). Through art, they become the metastable natures that they are. They are solid, and yet they flow. They achieve the tranquil enjoyment of materialist philosophy by aesthetic means. Here we see Lucretius at his most original, swerving away from the rationalist limitations of Epicureanism.

This chapter aims to show that human culture was taught to humans by nature but that humans also made several interpretive errors with the invention of states, religion, and war. One significant consequence of this, according to Lucretius, is that nature and culture are not radically separate at all. Culture is an emergent and immanent aspect of nature, or at least this is what I would like to show through a close reading of lines 5.1100–457.

The Birth of Civilisation

Lucretius jumps from Palaeolithic and Neolithic humans to the rise of kings without transition or explanation. However, we could locate this transition at around 3500 BCE in ancient Mesopotamia or Sumer. There, the first kings began to establish enclosed cities and fortress strongholds to direct, control, and provide protection and refuge [*praesidium perfugiumque*] for their populations, and to divide up flocks and fields and distribute them according to the appearance, intelligence, and strength of the inhabitants (5.1108–11).

The aim of early kings, priests, and aristocracy was to gather the wild flows of nature and confine them in a single arc or walled citadel. The origin of civilisation is the fear of nature's turbulence, and the attempt to secure a space against its swerves with the straight lines [*reges*] of walls and fences. This is a significant contrast with the roaming and wandering bacchants of earlier times. A hierarchy of moral virtues now replaced the verbal agreement among equals. Rulers divided the earth and animals.

The city is walled off from the countryside, the powerful from the weak. Nature's abundance and excess are constrained around 'scarce' objects that are centralised and protected. Kings increasingly prefer the relative stasis of the fixed urban structure to open mobility. Then 'property was invented and gold discovered', and the single value of wealth replaced the moral aristocracy (5.1113–15). Civilisation resisted the swerve at every turn.

Lucretius pauses here to explicitly condemn social values (moral or financial) in favour of the 'true' wealth of a human being, which 'is to live modestly [*parce*] with a calm mind [*aequo animo*], for never is there want of a little' (5.1119). In this political context, the word *aequo* recalls the *aequum misererier omnis* (5.1023) of social equality largely agreed upon by earlier humans. Lucretius thus emphasises, with the Latin word *aequo*, the twofold character of *individual* and *collective* peace and moderation. It is hard to be calm and enjoy the arts and beauty of nature when others around you are not equally able to enjoy them as well.

Mental calmness and pleasure do not occur in a vacuum, as Epicurus knew. Pleasure is a necessarily social project and requires some form of commune like Epicurus' garden where the assumption of equality prevails. There is, in other words, no ethics without politics. There is no wisdom without equality. In particular, as Marx would later emphasise, social hierarchies based on wealth are even more abstract and absurd because they are distinct from the qualities of nature. Wealth acquisition also has an inverse relationship to the *aequo omnis* or 'calm pleasures of equal beings'. The more wealth one gains, the more one has to worry about that wealth, and the more others have to worry about theirs. Wealth acquisition is both unequal and requires all kinds of 'empty cares' and strivings that surpass the much simpler domain where 'never is there want of a little'. Nature, for Lucretius, provides us with modest abundance.

The basis of civilisation, according to Lucretius, is the acquisition of fame and power [*potentes*] so that 'good fortune would stand fast on a firm foundation' [*fundamento stabili fortuna*] against the turbulence and indeterminacy of nature (5.1122–8).

et placidam possent opulenti degere vitam –
nequiquam, quoniam ad summum succedere honorem
certantes iter infestum fecere viai,
et tamen e summo, quasi fulmen, deicit ictos
invidia interdum contemptim in Tartara taetra,
invidia quoniam, ceu fulmine, summa vaporant
plerumque et quae sunt aliis magis edita cumque

and they with their wealth would be able to lead a smooth life –
all in vain, since struggling to advance to the height of honor
they saw to it that the path of their life was filled with danger,
and yet envy, like a thunderbolt, sometimes strikes and hurls
them down with great scorn into bitter Tartarus,

since envy, like a thunderbolt, usually sets ablaze
the heights and whatever rises up higher than the rest.

The goddess Fortuna is a goddess of flows, of rivers, of the sea, and of indeterminacy. No one can control her movement. The Romans celebrated her by taking a gambling boat down the River Tiber to her temple and participating in a Mystery cult related to the twin goddess Demeter/Persephone worshipped at Eleusis.[2] Fortuna even shared a Roman temple complex with Mater Matuta, whom Lucretius invoked earlier. The Romans worshipped Fortuna as a primordial mother goddess but also sought to master her with gifts. Urbanisation tried to control the flows so those in power could live a 'smooth life' [*placidam possent opulenti degere vitam*].

But it was all in vain! The acts that were necessary to secure and straighten out the twisted and turbulent flows of nature forced humans into a struggle filled with danger and unnecessary difficulty. Humans cannot and will not master nature. The effort at mastery is motivated by fear and envy, and plagued by self-inflicted misery. The hubris of building the city on the hill and trying to play god over nature and other humans only makes it more likely that one will be struck by lightning, Lucretius remarks. The higher the tower, the more precarious the perch (5.1129–33).

ut satius multo iam sit parere quietum
quam regere imperio res velle et regna tenere.
proinde sine incassum defessi sanguine sudent,
angustum per iter luctantes ambitionis,
quandoquidem sapiunt alieno ex ore petuntque
res ex auditis potius quam sensibus ipsis,
nec magis id nunc est neque erit mox quam fuit ante.

Thus it is much better to keep a quiet life
than to desire supreme command over things and to rule kingdoms.
Therefore let them get exhausted and sweat blood in vain,
struggling with difficulty along the narrow path of ambition,
since their wisdom comes from another's mouth and they are seeking
things more from hearsay than from their own sensations,
nor does it work better now or in the future than it did in the past.

Lucretius rejects the whole mission of civilisation along with the 'narrow' [*angustum*] 'struggle' [*luctantes*] of imperialism, hierarchy, and domination.

By contrast, the quiet [*quietum*] life is one of simple and meandering pleasures, not one of hard labour or military conquest.

True wisdom comes from the senses and not from the mouths of others. So, instead of competing to accumulate wealth and power with and over others, the senses provide all the simple pleasures one needs. Ambition is suffering because it assumes a lack as its motivation for achievement. One of the critical ideas of Lucretius' philosophy of natural history is that it lacks nothing, not even death. It is abundance and excess, dissipation and iteration. That we have a life at all is a gift, and any pleasure we might have is above and beyond what it would have been had we not existed.

It is not just that Lucretius does not like kings or merchants. He thinks the entire project of cities and states is about division, hierarchy, ambition, and imperialism. In contrast to the more centripetal gatherings of early humans around their sacred groves and fountains in the woods, Lucretius describes the next historical period as a centrifugal movement where power, once accumulated, radiates out from a central king.

Lucretius' description of ethical and political life as one of free, modest, and quiet enjoyment does not seem to be compatible with any state that has existed in history. His most detailed description of what we might call the good life comes only at the end of Book V and sounds very much like an artistic version of Epicurus' commune of friends.

Eventually, it's not clear when, Lucretius says, as the disparity between the powerful and powerless increased, the 'kings were killed', then trampled [*pedibus*] by social disorder [*turbasque*] (5.1141). Unfortunately, by this time society was quite individualistic, and 'each sought power and the highest station for himself' (5.1142). All they could imagine was rule by powerful individuals. However, instead of fixing this terrible idea, they tried to mitigate it by creating magistrates, statutes, and laws. So people, Lucretius says, followed laws and did good things out of fear of punishment. Since 'the fear of punishment taints the prizes of life', they made laws [*legibus*] so that violence and harm would encircle [*circumretit*] perpetrators like a net and turn their violence back upon them in the form of punishment.

This is an unusual and hardly utopian image of a law-governed society. For Lucretius, legal societies, in contrast to centripetal ones and centrifugal ones, function more like a tensional web of relations between individuals. Individuals decide not to break the law, not because they do not want to but because they fear punishment. Law is the internalisation of fear within a fraternal field of individuals. Their spontaneous action [*sponte sua*] is now mediated directly by the laws (5.1147).

The Birth of Religion

The rise of legal bonding and binding emerged alongside another central idea of social binding: religion. According to Lucretius, religion and the gods were historical inventions. Humans had not always had religion or known of the gods. 'Now what cause made the divinity of the gods known' (5.1161–2)? The fact that the gods have a historical origin based on human minds and the spread of their ideas [*pervulgarit*] indicates that, for Lucretius, the gods occur as images in our minds and do not exist in-between worlds.

Lucretius places the birth of the idea of gods and religion directly after the invention of law and statutes because the two share a common structure. Lucretius defines *legibus* and *religio* as bindings or enclosures that net or trap people through fear and punishment. Law and religion also bind individuals to states and priests. The spread of gods and rites is thus related to the spread of the fear of punishment [*insitus horror*].

Law and religion are part of the moral imagination. Law relies on abstract and general virtues that people must conform to for fear of punishment. Religion projects these ideal virtues (and vices) on to the gods and suffers their rewards and punishments. In both cases, there is an attempt to explain and control the turbulent movements of nature. The gods cause the world to move, while laws express a desire to freeze and fix the foundations of human and natural movement. Laws and gods are mechanisms of control born of a fear of nature and a fear of death. Humans used religion and legislation to stop the flow of matter and secure life, morality, and causality. But it was all in vain, and they paid a heavy price for it.

When humans imagined a set of virtues such as strength, intelligence, and courage, they also imagined figures possessing these virtues. The more they believed and saw these figures in their dreams and waking imaginations, the more the figures remained constant. Given such virtues, these figures would surely be untroubled by death.

The gods were, according to Lucretius, ideas that took on a permanence through repetition. They are, like everything else, metastable patterns whose forms are 'held in place' [*forma manebat*]. The danger, though, is that the images of the gods 'get under our feet' [*subpeditatur*] and trip us up. This image also recalls the way *religio* oppresses us by standing with its foot on our neck in subjection (1.62) and the importance Lucretius grants to standing up and trampling it under our feet [*pedibus subiecta*] (1.78). Materialist philosophy shows us that there is no underworld under our feet [*Acherusia templa*] (3.27).

Just as kings sought 'refuge' [*perfugiumque*] (5.1109) behind the centralised accumulation of wealth and power inside cities, so people sought explanatory 'refuge' [*perfugium*] (5.1186) in the gods as causal agents of 'the workings of the sky and the varying seasons' (5.1183). Humans 'maintained that all things are directed by their [the gods'] will' (5.1187). Urbanism, law, and religion are three historical ways of trying to escape nature's turbulence and arrest its indeterminacy. God is a 'jurist-priest-king'.[3] He is three expressions of a single general framework that assumes that the universe is created by a god and guided by divine laws just as humans are ruled by kings and governed by social laws.

People worshipped kings and gods with the same fear and supplication. Piety [*pietas*], Lucretius warns, has been understood as self-abasement. Humans cover their heads, lie prostrate on the ground, and sacrifice to the gods (5.1195–201), just as they kneel before their kings in fear. Kings live in constant fear of being removed from power because the more people they rule, the more likely is a revolt. So, just as kings seek refuge in their walled throne rooms with their backs to the wall, the kings of kings (the gods) seek an ultimate refuge beyond the world entirely. The gods are just images of kings who never die. They are divine monarchs, the source of all causal and moral law.

However, according to Lucretius, real *pietas* is to 'look upon everything with a tranquil mind' (5.1203). When we look up at 'the heavenly temple of the great universe' [*caelestia mundi templa super stellisque*] (5.1204–5), we should not worry that there is an all-powerful will that is ruling it and us. This will make us afraid and feel submissive to its arbitrary rule. Instead, we should calmly and gently go with the flow of natural processes, satisfied and content with all that nature has given to us in her abundance. We are not slaves to kings and gods or separate from them and nature. We grew out of the earth like seeds from a plant.

Religion 'attacks the split mind' [*temptat enim dubiam mentem*] with doubts when we lack a naturalistic explanation [*rationis*] for the 'turbulent motion' [*solliciti motus*] of things (5.1211). We are tempted to think there is a difference between an active cause (a divine will) and a passive effect (material nature). The split mind is the dualistic mind.

This is why Lucretius' naturalistic and material explanation, as speculative as it may be regarding celestial dynamics, is part of a more ethical way of life. He knows he may be wrong about some of the patterns and rhythms of the universe, but he did not resort to unprovable metaphysical claims that leave humans cut off from nature, passive, and cowering in fear. The knowledge that nature has a real swerving agency that cannot be fully known and predicted by science may sound paradoxical. What could the knowledge of indeterminacy possibly amount to? It is a brilliant ethical and historical move that frees humans from the determinate wills of gods, laws, kings, and fear. Historical indeterminacy means that control and domination by fear will always fail and fall apart.

If the world were utterly random, it would produce 'learned helplessness' and constant anxiety. However, if laws, gods, or anything else determined the world, we would feel a similar fear and helplessness. The only escape is the third way of *indeterminacy* and the *swerve*.

De Re Metallica

Metallurgy, like all things, came from nature. For Lucretius, humans generally do not do anything radically different from what nature does in a more general way. Language, fire, cooking, metallurgy, weaving, singing, and painting are variations in processes that pre-existed humans. Human culture is, therefore, entirely natural and material, for Lucretius. Even our absurd beliefs in laws, gods, and kings that rule nature as passive stuff is itself a habit based on our observation of sensuous patterns in nature.

Just as nature showed humans how to use fire and cook, it showed them how to cook metal and mould it into forms. Metallurgy also teaches them about the nature of things. Either by lighting, fire hunting, or agricultural burning, humans noticed that when the ground was heated by fire,

manabat venis ferventibus in loca terrae
concava conveniens argenti rivus et auri,
aeris item et plumbi, quae cum concreta videbant
posterius claro in terra splendere colore,
tollebant nitido capti levique lepore,
et simili formata videbant esse figura
atque lacunarum fuerant vestigia cuique,

tum penetrabat eos posse haec liquefacta calore
quamlibet in formam et faciem decurrere rerum,
et prorsum quamvis in acuta ac tenvia posse

there flowed out in molten veins and collected together
into hollow pockets of the earth a stream of silver and gold,
and likewise of copper and lead. When they saw these afterward
congealed together and shining on the ground in vivid colors,
they lifted them up, captivated by their smooth and shiny charm,
and saw that they had been formed with a shape similar to
the imprints of the hollow pockets each had possessed before.
Then it hit them that these things that were liquefied
by heat could assume any form or shape of things,
even right up to being able to be shaped and pounded. (5.1255–63)

Metallurgy is an image of a kinetic and materialist ontology. It is an image of history in miniature that no doubt struck humans as revealing something critical about the nature of matter. In the dissipation of energy (fire), matter becomes liquid and flows out into veins like the rivulets of the sacred spring and tree in the numinous grove where humans first gathered. Out of the earth came a material knowledge of shape-changing matter in motion. Matter melts, flows, and then gathers together into little pools and congeals into things. Eventually, it heats up again and flows away, leaving a trail or track [*vestigia*] of its material history. This is the metallurgic nature of things. Form [*figura*] is only a metastable by-product traced by matter in continual motion.

Metallurgy can be used to make tools or weapons of war. When humans chose to create war, so 'sad discord begot one thing from another' (5.1305). Through warfare, humans turned nature against itself. Nature experiments, but some human experiments lead to catastrophe when they are undertaken with a mistaken understanding of humankind's place in nature. Lucretius says warfare ends poorly in contrast to the better strategy of weaving and grafting described below.

In battle, they captured wild animals and used them as weapons, Lucretius says. The famous Lucretius scholar Cyril Bailey calls this 'perhaps the most astonishing paragraph in the poem'.[4] What is so astonishing about this passage is that Lucretius' poetic description of the animals' resistance and indiscriminate attack upon everyone on the battlefield resonates with his portrayal of nature's swerve. The poet says that 'The lionesses *hurled* their enraged bodies around with a leap everywhere, and aimed for the faces of those coming at them', creating 'turbulence' [*turbabant*] (4.1314). The bulls threw [*iaciebant*] (5.1318) their own riders and crushed them underfoot [*pedibusque*] (5.1323) and the horses kicked bodies into the air 'spreading' [*diffugiebat*] (5.1338) them all over the field. Wild animals, like matter, swerve, fly, flow, and scatter all over the place, creating turbulence and mixtures [*permixtasque*] (5.1329) that cannot be mastered by kings, soldiers, and organised warfare.

Weaving and Grafting as an Image of the Cosmos

This same turbulence is also the source of one of nature's most important gifts to humans: weaving and planting seeds. Nature, Lucretius says, 'compelled, summoned, or drove' [*coëgit*] men to begin spinning wool [*lanam*] before women. Eventually, however, 'strict' [*severi*] farmers said it was an unmanly activity that should be replaced by the 'suffering of hard labor in the fields' [*durum sufferre laborem*] (5.1272). For Lucretius, this is regrettable, since the point of life is not hard labour but pleasures, which do not hurt anyone. Nature drove men to weave, but they turned away from it.

Similarly, nature spread her swarming seeds on the ground during the proper planting season and taught humans how to sow. This is yet another poetic image of the nature of things. Trees let loose swerving, swarming [*examina*], and falling [*caducae*] sprouts [*pullorum*] in the proper season (5.1361–4). Just as matter flows, falls, and sprouts in rhythmic cycles, so do plants. In this way, nature was also the first teacher of the great mystery of creation and destruction. Most importantly, nature taught humans that this dissipation, dissemination, and iteration of swarming differences gives great *pleasure* (5.1365–9).

> *unde etiam libitumst stirpis committere ramis*
> *et nova defodere in terram virgulta per agros,*
> *inde aliam atque aliam culturam dulcis agelli*
> *temptabant, fructusque feros mansuescere terra*
> *cernebant indulgendo blandeque colendo,*

And thus too it was pleasing to graft stems onto branches
and to plant new shoots into the earth throughout the fields.
Then they tried successive methods of cultivating their dear little

plots and saw wild fruits grow milder in the earth
by being tenderly looked after and lovingly cultivated.

This passage evokes more than just agricultural utility. Planting entails
pleasure [*libitumst*], tenderness, and love for growing seeds, shoots, and
plants. Nature taught humans how to love and enjoy reproducing plants
as much as plants themselves enjoy reproducing themselves. This a fascinating story of symbiosis and the co-evolution of desire across species.
Plants showed humans how to cultivate them and rewarded humans
with larger and milder fruits. This, in turn, increased human fertility.

Lucretius' history of planting contrasts palpably with his history of
farming. In the case of agriculture, men valorised masculine hardness,
suffering, and physical labour. By contrast, the origins of planting and
grafting are all about mutual pleasure, dear little plots tenderly cared
for and lovingly cultivated. The more tenderly humans cared for wild
plants, the more tenderly the plants responded. Lucretius' description
suggests that the hardness of masculine labour has strayed away from
the earlier path of more natural and loving cultivation methods.

Planting is not about the linear and hard exploitation of the land but
the swarming plurality of seeds. The more general philosophical wisdom
here is that pleasure comes through *dissipation* and *diversity*. With this
image, Lucretius compares the act of growing seeds to the spreading
out of the cosmos. The Latin word *examina*, for example, means both
'to pour out a swarming multitude' and 'to consider or examine'. So
when humans consider or examine nature, they see and participate in a
dissipative multitude and gain pleasure from its swarming diversity. The
Latin word *semina* (seeds) is, after all, a key term that Lucretius uses to
describe the flow of matter.

To consider or think, in this sense, is a dissipative act done at the
right time [*tempestiva*]. Spreading out is not just about survival; it is about
sharing the pleasure of dissipation and dissemination with the vegetal
world. Instead of the plantation model of farming (forced labour, irri-
gation rows, mono-cropping, and forest clearing), nature brings about
pleasure through swerving and swarming. Before the 'serious' and 'sober'
instrumentalisation of plant cultivation, it was a joy and a pleasure.

Aesthetic Communism

Lucretius concludes Book V with one of the most beautiful passages in the book on the origin of the arts and their social function. His critique of religion, kings, and states is explicit throughout, but one wonders, what is Lucretius' alternative society? Lines 5.1379–410 are as close as we get to an explicit description of what Lucretius imagines the good life to be.

Art precedes human beings. Human art is only one expression of the arts of nature continued by other means. Lucretius writes that 'humans imitated the clear-toned voices of birds with their mouths', 'and the

Figure 7.1 Titian, *The Bacchanal of the Andrians* (1523–26). The island of Andros was so favoured by Bacchus that a stream flew with wine. Gods, men, and children celebrate the effects of wine, whose consumption, in Philostratus' words, makes men rich, dominant, generous to their friends, handsome and four cubits high. A nude nymph lies in the foreground, and Silenus in the background. Wikimedia Commons.

breeze whistling through the hollows of reeds first taught country people to blow on hollow hemlock stalks' (5.1379–80). He also says that 'the seasons of the year painted colorful flowers on the green-growing grass' (5.395–6). Nature painted with colours and sang with voice and instrument. Nature, over 'time gradually draws each and every thing into the open and technique throws it out [*erigit*] onto the shores of light' (5.1389).

Nature tends to spread out and dissipate into the open over time. As it does so, it teaches [*docuere*] everything how to do this. With practice, method, and technique, humans took up these sounds like a baton in a relay race and spread out their own sounds. Art, poetry, and music brought humans the two highest ethical aims of pleasure and tranquillity in a turbulent world (5.1390–8).

> *Haec animos ollis mulcebant atque iuvabant*
> *cum satiate cibi; nam tum sunt omnia cordi,*
> *saepe itaque inter se prostrati in gramine molli*
> *propter aquae rivom sub ramis arboris altae*
> *non magnis opibus iucunde corpora habebant,*
> *praesertim cum tempestas ridebat et anni*
> *tempora pingebant viridantis floribus herbas,*
> *tum ioca, tum sermo, tum dulces esse cachinni*
> *consuerant; agrestis enim tum musa vigebat,*

These songs soothed their minds and gave delight
when they had eaten sufficiently for then all things are pleasing.
And so often, reclining beside one another in the soft grass
beside a stream of water beneath the branches of a tall tree,
and at not great expense they delightfully entrained their bodies,
especially when the weather smiled down and the seasons of the year
painted colorful flowers on the green-growing grass.
Then joking around, then conversation, then sweet laughter often
occurred. For then the sylvan muse was alive and thriving,

According to Lucretius, at the start of Book V, the most valuable achievement of materialist philosophy was that it soothed people's minds from their fear of punishment by the gods. Once we have the modest material conditions for aesthetic enjoyment (food and safety), art and music can soothe the body and mind and bring delight and pleasure [*iuvabant*]. Eating is also a sensual pleasure that affirms our fundamental energetic relationship with the rest of nature as a process of spreading and dissipating motion.

What is it about art and philosophy that allows them to fulfil this highest ethical aim? First of all, it is a crucial materialist point, echoed later by Karl Marx and Virginia Woolf, that the conditions for an ethical life of peace and pleasure are food, shelter, and safety. Both were careful readers of Lucretius and saw that the conditions of communism required a minimal amount of shared labour and equality to keep everyone alive and safe.

After this, however, how are we to spend our time? Here is where Lucretius swerves away from Epicurus and consistently affirms the importance of aesthetic pleasure for an ethical life. Epicurus may have been happy to drink water and contemplate the gods, but Lucretius, Marx, and Woolf felt that art, poetry, and music were *essential* to ethical life. One must have peace but also *pleasure* and *sensuous* enjoyment.[5]

This is why they all shared a radical ethics and politics against all forms of domination and war. The subversive goal of liberation was to support the maximum amount of free creative activity and aesthetic enjoyment. For Marx, the purpose of communism was not mere survival but to express one's life in pleasure. 'The less you eat, drink, buy books, go to the theatre or to balls, or to the pub, and the less you think, love, theorize, sing, paint, fence, etc. . . . The less you are . . . the less you express your life, the more you have, the greater is your alienated life.'[6] Woolf writes poignantly that 'one cannot think well, love well, sleep well, if one has not dined well'.[7] 'Intellectual freedom depends upon material things. Poetry depends upon intellectual freedom. And women have always been poor.'[8] However, Epicurus said that music was not beneficial and that poetry was useless and of no philosophical value.[9] This is a crucial difference between Lucretian and Epicurean philosophies.

The more radically materialist position is that of Lucretius (and his lineage through Marx and Woolf), for whom art and sensation can produce the same tranquillity as rational philosophy and a more extensive range of pleasures than philosophy alone. In other words, knowledge, for Lucretius, is not just mental and rational but also bodily and material. Art, including nature's art of birdsong and wind, thus acts as a form of knowledge *through the body*. Art and philosophy are both material and sensuous but proceed by different techniques. Neither is separate or superior to the other for Lucretius.

But why do art and music soothe our minds and bodies? The answer lies in their *material historical* origins, according to Lucretius. Humans learned everything from nature, including language, wisdom, art, science, and technology. This is why Lucretius says that speaking, weaving, planting, and art all bring *pleasure*. Nature pleases us with its endless iterative dissipations. It is always repeating itself but with ever novel twists and mesmerising singularities. When humans iteratively innovate with what nature makes, they are not just mimicking it. They are doing what nature does in the way that nature taught them. It pleases us to live and make as nature does through differential repetitions.

The iteration of poetic images in this passage on art is worth reading carefully. Lucretius says that human bodies are *prostrati* across the soft grass (5.1392). *Prostrati* derives from the verb meaning 'to strew before, spread out, cast down, throw to the ground, overthrow, or prostrate'. This exact term and image was invoked earlier at (2.29) and paralleled matter's spreading or flowing out in pleasurable dissipation. In this position, the human body shows its dendritic features dramatically. Its limbs are flowing out from its core, and from those limbs its fingers and toes spread out.

The next iteration of this image occurs in the 'stream of water' flowing alongside the spread-out bodies. River water flows and dissipates in dendritic rivulets and whirling eddies, just like the spreading limbs of the human body, whose veins iterate the formation of river tributaries. The river is a body spreading its limbs out across the soft grass just as the human body is a river doing the same.

The human and river spread out under that other vast dendritic figure of iterative dissipation: 'the branches of a tall tree' (2.30; 5.936; 5.1393). The running water beneath the tall tree recalls the first numinous scene where the bubbling spring and sylvan grove drew humans together. The spring flows out, and the tree flows up, both in a dendritic pattern that is singular and patterned. The tree spreads its limbs up and out into the open like the river and the human body. Each shows the other what they are insofar as they share a similar dendritic form. The movement of matter bridges the division between biological and physical processes.[10]

'And at not great expense they delightfully entrained their bodies [*corpora habebant*]' (5.1394), with the rhythms of iterative dissipation around them. Humans lay spread out on the ground, 'supported, held, cared for, and entrained with' [*habebant*] the processes that they are, namely, dendritic dissipation of water, plants, wind, and earth. This is not a strictly rational or mental activity but a material and physical feeling of becoming the earthly creatures that they are through sensation. The rhythm of the music entrains their bodies. The musical structure itself entrains with the rhythmic structure of the seasons, days, animal sounds of the forest, and the wind through the trees. Humans and nature are not one but rather multiple, like waves within waves, each singular but folded into the others, endlessly tessellated.

Lucretius is careful to stress here, for the sober Epicurean reader, that this sensuous entrainment and delight does not require any 'great expense'. If it did, then the Epicurean would be quick to respond that the pain of striving for it and maintaining it would outweigh the pleasure, and we ought to go back to contemplating the gods in silence.

The final lines of this passage recall the images of spring weather and fresh flowers from the proems of Books I–IV. In particular, the phrase 'weather smiled down' [*tempestas ridebat*] invokes the beautiful Homeric image of a springtime Mt Olympus at 3.22 that quickly turned into an ecstatic visionary experience. After Lucretius 'drinks' Epicurus' philosophy, he has an epiphanic vision of beautiful springtime weather and the whole of nature laid out before his eyes. He then begins to shake and tremble with a profound ecstasy and divine rapture (3.28–9).

The pure 'delight' of the aesthetic experience here in Book V is about more than enjoyment. It is an ethical delight in the tranquil and iterative dissipation of the universe. Nature completes this beautiful scene with 'painted colorful flowers on the green-growing grass' (5.1396). Natural and human art are folds in the same fabric. Human art expresses the same fractal processes we find so beautiful in nature. The river flows along, dissipating energy like our bodies as we eat and pass matter through their tubes. Music, too, moves through our bodies and dance entrains our manifold.

According to Epicurus, 'pleasure cannot be increased as soon as pain caused by want has been removed, but only varied'.[11] However, Lucretius thinks the limit of healthy pleasure is higher than not being hungry. Nature taught humans to speak and enjoy it, 'joking around, then conversation, then sweet laughter' (5.1403). Joking around is hardly Epicurean wisdom, and yet Lucretius ascribes critical importance to *laughter*. Just as the river babbles joyfully and the birds sing with delight, humans gossip, joke, and laugh. Laughter is a joyful expression of unnecessary cosmic dissipation. It is the human animal's 'joy before death', as the French philosopher George Bataille wrote.[12]

Fittingly, Lucretius invokes at this moment the numinous sylvan spirit that first brought humans together long ago (5.948), 'For then the sylvan muse was alive and thriving' (5.1398). The muse thrives through the dissipation and waste of aesthetic enjoyment. Although we are a long way from the first human gatherings, something numinous is still iterated in the primal scene of human art and speech by the river under the tree.

For Lucretius, it was not through reason that humans 'invented' art, but rather through pleasure and playful experimentation with nature (5.1399–404).

tum caput atque umeros plexis redimire coronis
floribus et foliis lascivia laeta monebat,
atque extra numerum procedere membra moventes
duriter et duro terram pede pellere matrem;
unde oriebantur risus dulcesque cachinni,
omnia quod nova tum magis haec et mira vigebant,

Then pleasing playfulness taught them to encircle their heads
and shoulders with festive crowns woven from leaves and flowers,
and to step forward without rhythm, moving their limbs
clumsily and with clumsy foot pounding mother earth.
From this smiles and sweet laughter blossomed, since all
these things then bloomed, new and wondrous.

Seeing the playfulness and pleasure of the way trees spread and grow, humans wanted to play too and so wanted to become like trees. So they wove [*plexis*] leaves and flowers around their heads to celebrate the festival of nature's woven excess (5.1399). In contrast to the perfectly circular crowns of kings trampled underfoot, the woven and spiralled flower crown is the one Lucretius says he seeks as he wanders through the mountains of the Muses (1.929; 4.1–4).

Just as language begins with stuttering, dancing begins with stepping clumsily without rhythm. The movement of limbs [*membra moventes*] produces joy and laughter. Dance is the blooming of the body. It is the unfolding of the universe into something novel and wondrous. Here the image of *membra* returns, and we recall that the cosmos is limbs of limbs. Putting these two images together, we get a powerful picture. As the universe spreads, it unfolds and moves its appendages in experimentation, like the limbs of a tree moving in the wind. Humans dance the many-limbed experimental dance of the cosmos.

The scene parallels Lucretius' description of his poetic journey to the mountains of the Muses to find new springs to drink and fresh flowers to weave into a crown for his head. The poet is then stabbed in the heart with Dionysus' thyrsus, and his mind begins to 'bloom' [*mente vigenti*] (1.925), just like the 'blooming' dancers [*vigebant*] (5.1404). In the two poetic scenes, we have an image of pleasure [*dulcesque*], but also creativity [*nova*], and wisdom. We are learning how to do what nature does: to dissipate, to go with the flow, to bloom, experiment, and pass away without fear. Art, Lucretius says, brings 'solace' [*solacia*] (5.1405), just as philosophy and ethics do.

A History of Pleasure

Have we indeed gained any more pleasure today than the forest children dancing by the river thousands of years ago? Lucretius says no. This is because one can only have so much pleasure before it produces more pain than it is worth. Also, later pleasures transform our capacities and feelings towards previous pleasures.

The history of desire is not linear or progressive. Each subsequent addition transforms the whole. This is why utilitarianism does not work. We cannot calculate the greatest pleasure for the greatest number of people because pleasure is continually mutating and transforming our relationship to all previous desires. We do not know what new pleasures we are capable of, nor technically what old ones we enjoyed. 'And the better thing discovered later usually destroys the former things and changes our feelings toward anything old' (5.1414–15). The only real history of pleasure is one of continual experimentation without fixed objective conditions of judgement. The only transhistorical pleasure is the process of inventing new pleasures, the pleasure of the 'blooming' body and mind, as Lucretius puts it. History is a flower, filled with laughter, excess, and playfulness.

Lucretius is not a romantic about the past. Previous pleasures were not any better or worse than current ones because there is no objective standard. The criteria of pleasure are always historically immanent. Each age must try and experiment with diverse but non-destructive pleasures and see what they like. We cannot eliminate suffering, danger, and turbulence. It will only increase suffering to try. Gold and purple robes, Lucretius says, will not keep us any warmer than simpler ones. They may bring pleasure, but if that pleasure commits us to mining, imperialism, or envy, they are quickly not worth the hassle.

The techniques of pleasure and art only emerge step by step (5.1451–3).

carmina picturas et daedala signa polita,
usus et impigrae simul experientia mentis
paulatim docuit pedetemptim progredientis

songs, paintings, and skillfully worked polished statues:
these were gradually revealed by practice along with the experimentation
of a quick mind to humans progressing step-by step.

History proceeds dialectically, with each new step transforming the immanent conditions of the whole process. Just as the universe proceeds step by step [*pedetemptim*], so does art (5.1453). Neither the past nor the future can be known *tout court*. 'Therefore our age is unable to determine what happened before, except if historical method somehow shows [*monstrat*] traces' (5.1446–7).

We thus reach a paradox. History occurs step by step, but each step changes all the previous steps. We have entered the Minoan labyrinth. To show history, we must also walk step by step back over the earlier footprints. This is what Lucretius precisely says he has done with Epicurus' footprints. By walking over them, he has changed them. History is thus, fittingly, *monstrous* [*monstrat*]. Writing history creates something new and hybrid between the past and the present.

Conclusion

Lucretius' history of the present reveals that humans have, unfortunately, increasingly cut up and dominated nature. In an attempt to secure their complete safety, power, and destructive pleasures, they have forgotten that some pleasures also produce suffering. The dangers of nature can only be avoided to a certain degree before avoidance itself becomes a danger. History is not linear or even circular, but a turbulent vortex. To live well is to travel the spiral and live a metastable life.

Notes

1 Michel Serres, *The Birth of Physics*, trans. David Webb and William Ross, 2nd edn (Lanham, MD: Rowman and Littlefield International, 2018), 156.

2   Michael Gagarin (ed.), *The Oxford Encyclopedia of Ancient Greece and Rome, Volume 1* (Oxford: Oxford University Press, 2010), 212.

3   Georges Dumézil, *Mitra-Varuna: essai sur deux representations indo-européennes de la souveraineté*, 2nd edn (Paris: Gallimard, 1948).

4   T. Lucreti Cari, *De Rerum Natura Libri Sex*, ed. Cyril Bailey (Oxford: Clarendon Press, 1947), ad 1308–49 (iii.l529f.).

5   See Thomas Nail, *Woolf: Moments of Becoming* (under review); and Thomas Nail, *Marx in Motion: A New Materialist Marxism* (Oxford: Oxford University Press, 2020).

6   Karl Marx, *Economic and Philosophic Manuscripts of 1844*, trans. and ed. Martin Milligan (Mineola, NY: Dover Publications, 2007), 119.

7   Virginia Woolf, *A Room of One's Own* (Orlando: Harcourt, 2013), 18.

8   Woolf, *A Room of One's Own*, 108.

9   Epicureans did not reject poetry entirely, but the greatest Epicurean pupil, Philodemus, says, in *On Poems*, that poetry is useless and of no philosophical value. 'This is in fact the line that Lucretius' contemporary Philodemus takes in *On Poems*: while accepting that poetry can give pleasure, he firmly denies that it can have any utility qua poetry. If it happens to be beneficial to the reader, that must be entirely the result of its content, and the same effect could presumably be achieved just as well if not better by employing prose-form.' Monica Gale, 'Lucretius and Previous Poetic Traditions', in Stuart Gillespie and Philip Hardie (eds), *The Cambridge Companion to Lucretius* (Cambridge: Cambridge University Press, 2012), 59–75, 73.

10   Something similar occurs in Empedocles: 'reasonable to expect them to behave in analogous fashion, particularly as Empedocles' panpsychism (frs. 103 and 110.10) erases the division between biological and physical processes.' Monica Gale, *Myth and Poetry in Lucretius* (Cambridge: Cambridge University Press, 1994), 64.

11   'Principal Doctrines of Epicurus', in *Diogenes Laertius: Lives of Eminent Philosophers, Volume II*, trans. R. D. Hicks (London: Heinemann, 1925), Book X, Section 144, no. 18.

12   Georges Bataille, 'The Practice of Joy before Death', in *Visions of Excess: Selected Writings, 1927–1939*, ed. Allan Stoekl, trans. Allan Stoekl, Carl R. Lovitt, and Donald M. Leslie Jr. (Minneapolis: University of Minnesota Press, 1985), 235–9 .

Book VI

Book VII

8. A Hymn to Ruin

We have reached the final book of *De Rerum Natura*. The world is now quickly unravelling [*dissoluat*] (6.598) before our eyes. History is coming to an end. We know from Book V that the world was born and that it will die. Since the birth of human history, we have lived in a world of natural beauty but also of wild beasts and danger. Animals taught us to sing (birds) but also tore us to shreds. The critical lesson of Book V is that nature made us from itself and unmakes us as well.

The error of human history is that we have tried to achieve complete safety and mastery over nature with walls, states, and gods. In this way, we have inflicted suffering on ourselves in vain. Nature tends towards dissolution with or without us, and there is nothing we can do to stop it. According to Lucretius, pushing against the material flow of history is a painful and pointless struggle that we should abandon.

In Book VI, the scope of nature's dissolution expands to the entire earth. In this chapter, I would like to focus on two critical lessons from the first half of Book VI. The first is that the same processes that wove [*texta*] (6.351) the world together also unweave it. Every unweaving is the condition for weaving something else, but increasingly less so until the world is entirely unwoven. Matter is indeterminate and swerving, for Lucretius, so other universes are possible, but that does not change the fact that this world will eventually unravel.

The second and related lesson from the first half of Book VI is that nature tends to 'be everywhere similar to itself' (6.542) in its patterns of creation *and destruction*. What are these patterns? They are the twin patterns of historical materialism: dissipation and iteration. Matter flows, spreads out, and dissipates. The optimal method of dissolution, however, is through folding and vortical turbulence. These are precisely the patterns we find in Lucretius' description of atmospheric and terrestrial processes.

This chapter argues that material history is similar to itself every-where in its patterns of iterative dissipation. Lucretius expresses this poetically with the mythology of the ancient Mystery religion.

Mother Athens

At the end of Book V, Lucretius left us at the 'highest pinnacle of the arts' [*artibus ad summum donec venere cacumen*] (5.1457). Instead of strug-gling in vain to dominate nature with walls, states, statutes, and religion, humans learned art, music, and poetry from nature and animals and continued them in their own way. The arts taught humans to move as history does. It taught them to experiment, step by step, go with the flow, and enjoy the dissipation and excess of their energies like the rivers and trees around them. However, a pinnacle is also a relatively unstable energetic point that can easily fall to a more stable lower energy level. Art and the knowledge of material history prepare us, as much as pos-sible, for what comes next: the turbulence of the decline.

Ancient Athens was an important historical site for naturalist wisdom for several reasons (6.1–6). Bright [*praeclaro*] Athens, Lucretius says, was the first to disseminate and spread [*dididerunt*] (6.2) the fruits of the earth (cereal grains). Just as Lucretius describes his poem as a 'scattering of seeds' [*disserere*] (1.54), and nature as spreading [*pandam*] (1.54) its seeds of matter [*semina*], Athens is also spreading its seeds. In doing so, Athens 'gave new life' [*recreaverunt*] (6.3) to humans. With her seeds, she fulfilled the basic material needs of her people. She was also the first to offer them the 'sweet solace of life' [*solacia dulcia vitae*] (6.4) when she birthed Epicurus. Epicurus spread the word [*disserere*] that the world is mortal, that there is no reason to fear death or the gods, and that pleasure is easy to attain. The truth 'poured' [*profudit*] (6.6) from his mouth like the dis-sipating streams by which humans once sat.

In Athens, Lucretius sees the full convergence of the mythopoetic and philosophical traditions. The knowledge of the agricultural grain cycle or 'Mystery religions' was married to the naturalism of materialist philosophy. Athens did not invent agriculture but was one of the first main grain-trading cities in the Mediterranean along with Knossos in Crete. From around 900 BCE onwards, Athens was a leading centre of commercial trading.[1]

Appropriately, Athens was also responsible for the spread of the grain religion of Demeter, passed down from Minoan Crete. Every year initiates would walk 'the sacred way' from Athens to Eleusis, just as the grain goddess Demeter searched for her lost daughter Persephone. They would fast and purge themselves in preparation to drink the *kykeon* or mixture, just as Demeter did in her mourning. Initiates of the Mystery religion would enter a darkened room and drink a psychoactive ergot-like beverage and see a vision of the goddess and the underworld. They would directly experience the darkness of death and be guided back to the brilliant light of rebirth by the hierophant who conducted the ceremony.[2] This was the single most important and widespread religious practice in the pan-Hellenic world.

Epicurus, along with many of his pupils, was an initiate into these Mysteries.[3] Many philosophers also appropriated the language and structure of the Mysteries. They used it as an image to describe the movement from dark ignorance to enlightened wisdom. Empedocles, one of Lucretius' heroes, uses this imagery, as does Lucretius (1.1114–17; 3.29–30). As Peta Fowler argues, the influence of the Mysteries is 'unmistakable' in *De Rerum Natura*.[4]

Just as in the Mysteries, nature spreads the seeds of new life only to return them to death in the underworld. The initiate of the Mystery is not a rational contemplator but 'someone who has seen' [*epóptē*] directly through a sensuous vision granted by the psychedelic beverage. The decomposing fungal ergot grain shows the initiate, appropriately, the creation and destruction process – the 'dissipative iteration' that defines nature. The truth 'pours out' [*profudit*] (6.6) of Epicurus' mouth as the *kykeon* pours out into the mouth of the initiate. The truth of the Mystery religion is not that there are gods who control creation and destruction but that there are natural processes of dissipation and iteration that we call Demeter, Persephone, and Hades. Epicurus gave us the naturalistic tools to understand the material and historical truth of this sacred myth. Athens is the birthplace where we begin our 'sacred journey' to Eleusis and the birthplace of Epicurus, in whose writings we can start to interpret the truth of this myth.

Lucretius thus invokes Athens as the third mother of matter to complete the triptych: earthly mother (Gaia), divine mother (Demeter), and human mother (Athens). In doing so, he brilliantly weaves Epicurus into the mythological world at the same time. When Demeter arrived at Eleusis, she took up residence as a nurse for the king's children. The eldest son Triptolemus was sick, and so Demeter nursed him back to health with her breast milk. She also taught him the art of grain

Figure 8.1 Votive plaque depicting elements of the Eleusinian Mysteries. Demeter offers the *cista mystica* or 'secret casket'. Persephone and the Iakchos hold torches leading the procession of initiates arriving at the sanctuary. All participants are crowned with laurels. Wikimedia Commons.

cultivation, which he spread to others, riding his chariot drawn by dragons.[5]

Here we have another iteration of the spiral meander in the twisting image of the serpent-dragons and the dissemination of seeds. Athens was one of the first significant disseminators of grain, but she got it from Triptolemus and Demeter. From here, Triptolemus also disseminated the Mystery religion of Demeter and Eleusis. The dragon chariot also connects Triptolemus to that other famous monster, the Python at Delphi. Eleusis and Delphi thus shared a wisdom of vortical dissipation.

Epicurus, then, is like the Triptolemus of mother nature spreading the seeds of the profound [*profudit*] (6.6) mystery: that the world is mortal and that we need not fear death. The 'sacred way' is a journey undertaken from the dark and obscure to the unfolded light *within things*. This is the original sense of the Greek word *theōríā* as 'a journey, or mission, a sight, spectacle, viewing, or beholding'. The deeper origins of pre-philosophical knowledge lie in the Minoan-inspired Mystery religion, and it is worth returning to those roots to recover a new materialist perspective.

Theory, in this sense above, is not some fixed thing or set of things to be known, but rather the *process of moving along a path*. The process of travelling is itself knowledge. This is why we find Lucretius wandering in the pathless mountains of the Muses, walking with us along various trails as our guide, and riding his chariot guided by the Muse of wisdom, beauty, and death: Calliope. Theory and history are not doctrines but processes to be experimentally 'laid open and uncovered in every part', step by step (3.29–30).

The Spring and the Tree

Athens was the 'pinnacle of the arts' because humans figured out how to provide regular food and moderate safety for themselves, making it possible to spend the rest of their time engaged in experimenting with new aesthetic pleasures. Athens is, for Lucretius, the modern version of the sylvan origins of art found near the spring and the tree.

It is worth pausing to consider the importance of the spring and the tree as material structures of knowledge in Lucretius' account. As I discussed in the previous chapter, the babbling spring and the sacred grove are twin images of iterative dissipation. The spring flows and spreads out, folding into bubbles, ripples, and eddies as it goes. The tree flows and spreads upwards into the sky, unfolding into branches and leaves with the seasons. These twin dramatic images of nature first drew humans together and continue to bring them together. They are twin images of beauty and wisdom. They show us what nature is up to across every scale of reality.

Athens was founded with two gifts from the gods: the olive tree from Athena and Poseidon's spring. Poseidon gave Athenians a stone, which he then struck with his trident to produce a spring. The Greeks associated springs with sacred stones and mountain baetyl rocks, depicted throughout Minoan religious artefacts, under sacred trees or in groves of sacred trees.

The oracle of Delphi also had its origins at a sacred grove of trees surrounding a babbling spring. At this site, a nymph named Telphusa oversaw and translated the oracular speech of the water. The oldest oracle in ancient Greece was that of Dodona. Dodona had an oracular oak tree that spoke when the wind blew through its leaves, near a sacred grove and a spring of fresh water. Also, according to the Homeric hymn, when Demeter arrived at Eleusis, she immediately went to the Well of the Dancing Flower Maidens under an olive tree.

Wells and springs are gateways to the underworld and were treated by the ancients as sources of wisdom. They were sources of creation and destruction. From their darkness comes a generous dissipation of energy – a source of life. Python, too, at Delphi, spoke from an opening in the earth. Demeter looked into the well at Eleusis, as if looking for Persephone, and found her mirror image reflected. The well thus unites mother and daughter, life and death. Inside the temple of Eleusis, the sacred groves of Minoan Crete appear as groups of stone columns. Outside, the initiates danced around the Well of the Beautiful Dances. The point is this: the spring/well and the tree/grove are the *material conditions* for food and drink, sites of social gathering, sacred sites of wisdom, and early sources of artistic inspiration. It is incredible how much cultural history owes to this simple material structure in nature. Culture is not distinct or isolatable from nature but is an expression of it.

Lucretius is aware of how this image of the tree and spring iterates through his history and leads us to Athens. He knows that the spring beneath the tree is a twofold image of creation and destruction. In his poem, no sooner does mother Athens give birth to Epicurus, but directly Lucretius invokes Epicurus' 'death' (6.7–8). Death is part of the dissemination of life. Now, in this context, Epicurus looks even more like a Dionysian figure. He is born from the seed mother but dies and then lives again through his teachings. If Epicurus is a god, as Lucretius satirically says in the proem of Book V, then he is a *dying god* who lives again through dissemination.

Figure 8.2 Well of Maidens at Eleusis.

What is the great wisdom of Epicurus, according to Lucretius? It is that 'he saw that nearly all things that need demands for living were ready close at hand for mortals, and that, to the extent they could [*proquam possent*], their life abides secure' (6.9–12). This is essentially the knowledge of the Mystery religions: abundance without fear. Nature provides everything in abundance – nourishment, wisdom, and even death. Nature gives us everything we need to be as safe as possible without increasing our suffering and infesting [*infestis*] (6.16) our lives with excessive cares, politics, wealth accumulation, wars, and religion. When death and destruction come, as they will for everything, we will have had our fill.

The Return of the Leaky Basket

The brilliance of Epicurus' ethics is twofold (6.17–23).

> *intellegit ibi vitium vas efficere ipsum,*
> *omniaque illius vitio corrumpier intus*
> *quae conlata foris et commoda cumque venirent,*
> *partim quod fluxum pertusumque esse videbat,*
> *ut nulla posset ratione explerier umquam;*
> *partim quod taetro quasi conspurcare sapore*
> *omnia cernebat, quaecumque receperat, intus,*

he realized then that the woven vessel itself made the flow,
all things within it pass through its braids, all
that are brought together and come from outside, even good things;
partly because he saw it was leaky and full of holes,
so that in no way could it ever be filled up,
partly because he perceived that it completely polluted, so to speak,
everything which it had taken in with a noxious taste.

First of all, there is a limit to how much pleasure and safety we can fea-
sibly attain without increasing suffering, anxiety, and social domination.
The human body and soul are embodied in a material world where
pleasure is not unconstrained. Lucretius does not think reality is infi-
nitely malleable by humans or social-linguistic structures. Humans are
relationally situated aspects of nature, and so are our pleasures.

For example, great wealth and pleasure can be accumulated by a few
people by enslaving the others, but 'these violent delights have violent
ends. And in their triumph die, like fire and powder. Which, as they
kiss, consume', as Shakespeare says.[6] Destructive pleasures require constant social domination, fear of retaliation, and pointless imperialism for
ever grander pleasures, when simpler ones would have sufficed. Since
pleasure is relative, for Lucretius, great excesses of it are totally futile
and mostly destructive. Extreme surpluses are even more pointless and
harmful if they are so massive that a lifetime is not enough for the owner
to enjoy them.

This is an essential thermodynamic point. Our bodies and souls are
woven from natural systems of energy that pass through us. Energy
comes into our bodies, reproduces them by circulating for a while,
and then flows out. Lucretius describes a whole kinetic theory of the
'woven' body and soul in Book III. This is essential background for
understanding the ethical point here (2.55–61; 3.555–7; 3.87–93).[7] The
fact that our entire being (body, mind, and soul) is a metastable state that
matter-in-motion continually flows through is not something that can
be changed. It is a material feature of our existence. Pleasures are not
objects or states that one attains or accumulates, but rather *processes* and
events that pass through us. Similarly, life is not something that we have
and can protect with certainty, but rather a material process that passes
through us and the world.

The proper name for the woven basket [*vas*] that Lucretius is describing is the Greek *calathus*. The *calathus* was a basket woven from reeds

Figure 8.3 Peter Paul Rubens, *Abundance* (c. 1630). Wikimedia Commons.

or sticks that typically held weaving supplies or performed as a harvest basket for grain, fruits, and vegetables. Originating from Minoan Crete, it was Demeter's cornucopia or 'horn of plenty'. It was Amalthea's horn of ambrosia that raised the baby Zeus on Crete. It is the perfect image of human existence because it is continually filled, drained, and refilled with agricultural abundance year after year. The leaky basket is the Athenian, grain-disseminating, human body.

Lucretius' affirmation of the *calathus* is also an explicit rejection of Plato's idea of the body as a watertight vessel that holds an immaterial soul. Instead, Lucretius gives us the Homeric image of a dripping sieve defined by movement, filtration, condensation, and entropy. The leaky soul is part of the constant process of life and death, creation and destruction. Even the *calathus* of the soul/body itself is not static, since Lucretius says that the soul and body are in a constant movement of weaving and unweaving.[8] This is also why he directly contrasts the *calathus* or woven vessel with the body as a 'cage' [*cavea*] (3.685).

What is pleasure then? It is the metastable process by which matter flows through the body within a given range. If the flows are excessive, the *calathus* overflows [*affluere*] (6.13) pointlessly. If the flows are insufficient, one may starve to death. The more significant point here is that because the flows of matter always alternate with pores or holes, there can be no absolute accumulation, total safety, or static pleasure. Everything passes through the body. Similarly, history cannot be understood developmentally or by states of accumulation, but rather by patterns of circulation. If nature is leaky, it is because history is also leaky. Everything runs right through, but always at a particular pace, and in vortical whorls. Unfortunately, so much of history and politics has been the vain Platonic quest to seal up an unsealable vessel.

This brings us to our second diagnostic of human suffering. If we expect to be able to catch and hold all the flows that pour into the *calathus* from outside, this will lead to a great hatred of such 'noxious' flows. We see them as 'polluting' our basket and grow to hate them and our 'defective' baskets. We may even try to renounce bodily pleasures altogether and become ascetics or idealists. We might see the world of flows as adverse to our abstract ideas of totality, unity, identity, immortality, and the gods.

The leaky basket is a fundamental starting point for thinking about materialist ethics, naturalism, and history. Starting from any other position leads to suffering and the hatred of nature. However, starting from

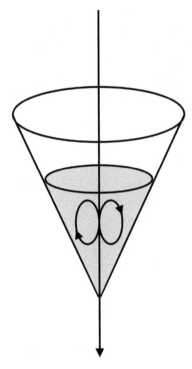

Figure 8.4 Calathus diagram.

the leaky basket presents its own unique challenge to accept, affirm, and enjoy the process of passage. For Lucretius, the sensible relationship to have to our thermodynamic situation goes with the flow and continually purges the mind and body [*purgavit pectora*] (6.24). Just as the material action of wormwood in Lucretius' honeyed cup is purgative, so is the material action of his ethics. One must learn to enjoy metastable pleasures and not think that 'an object is only ours when we have it'.[9]

Kinetic materialism is wormwood for the mind. It is a psychoactive purgative like Apollo's laurels or the *kykeon* of Eleusis that helps us let go of stability, stasis, formalism, and gods. It is like a turbulent snowstorm that covers over our snow-packed ruts. It enables us to wander the pathless mountains in search of new springs and flowers. It is akin to that metallurgical art of nature that melts matter, increases its entropy, and metamorphosises it into something new.

Lucretius taught us to relax and let the waters run through our basket joyfully. He did for philosophy what the Mysteries did for Greek religion. Demeter fasted, purged, and drank the *kykeon* to undergo the *katabasis* of death (as Persephone) and rebirth (as Dionysus). Lucretius' song showed us the birth of the world and now takes us down and 'unravels' it all before our eyes. We drink his song as he drinks from the unknown wild springs of the Muses. Our minds bloom like flowers, and our bodies shake with the divine ecstasy of nature spread out before us.

The Sacred Way

We start our descent to Eleusis on foot from Athens along 'the sacred way'. We start our philosophy from Epicurus, who first pointed out the little footpath towards the good (6.26–8).

> *exposuitque bonum summum quo tendimus omnes*
> *quid foret, atque viam monstravit, tramite parvo*
> *qua possemus ad id recto contendere cursu,*

> He set out what the highest good is towards which
> we all strive and showed the way by which, on a little
> footpath, we might struggle towards it without deviation.

The highest good is not a 'solid-state ethics' that we can achieve. It is only the 'most' [*summum*] pleasure we can have beyond which suffering and domination begin. This is not normative ethics by any means. History does not lead up to a correct answer or state of affairs. It only shows us that the 'sacred path' towards the good is, like nature herself, experimental. It proceeds step-by-step [*pedetemptim*] (5.1453) in walking collaboration with others. Endless new aesthetic pleasures await us, all without needing to destroy the earth and kill one another.

Ethics is something we struggle towards together. We make the path by walking it. However, if we make the path by walking, our swerves into the pathless forests do not deviate. We should recall that when Lucretius steps in Epicurus' footprints, he changes them. The highest good is to multiply and experiment with the broadest range of arts and pleasures under the conditions of material equality and safety. This is the path of Lucretius' 'aesthetic communism'.

Our bodies are 'gates' or 'doors' [*portis*], which the world 'runs through' [*occurri*]. Ethics is where we meet those flows and mediate their passage through us [*deceret*] (6.29–32). If we let them go through us too

Figure 8.5 Boundary marker delineating the limits of the Sacred Way in Athens, c. 520 BCE. At the end of the fifth century BCE, the original inscription was replaced by the words ΗΟΡΟΣ ΤΕΣ ΟΔΟ ΤΕΣ ΕΛΕΥΣΙΝΑΔΣΙ, 'Boundary stone of the road to Eleusis'. Wikimedia Commons.

fast, we enjoy nothing. If we try to retain everything, we will fail and exert too much effort and anxiety working against the flow. The optimal form of motion for a fluid to pass through a vessel is a vortex. This allows the fluid to pass through at a metastable rate of dissipation. Practically speaking, this means maintaining physical security for everyone without hierarchy or domination so that all are free to experiment with the most extensive range of sensations and pleasures.

The mere knowledge that 'everything flows' [*omnia migrant*] has enormous consequences. Instead of looking to static forms and gods for causal explanation, we can understand the world by its patterns of dissipation and iteration. There is no need to fear the dark like children or seek an external divine source of light to illuminate nature. If we walk the sacred path, step by step, nature illuminates itself from within (1.46–8; 2.5–61; 3.91–3; 6.39–41).

> *hunc igitur terrorem animi tenebrasque necessest*
> *non radii solis nec lucida tela diei*
> *discutiant, sed naturae species ratioque.*

Therefore this fear and darkness of the mind must be shattered
apart not by the rays of the sun and the clear shafts
of the day but by the external appearance and conditions of nature.

Lucretius mobilises yet another image from the ancient Mystery cult. The light of Eleusis was not the light of the sun. The ceremony took place in a darkened temple. The source of its light was the immanent capacity of the senses. When we drink the *kykeon* the truth is revealed not as external to us but as immanent with our senses. The truth is sensuousness. Nature shows itself to itself not through the mind but through the mutual exteriority of sensuous appearance.[10]

Awakening Calliope

The *kykeon* illuminates nature through sensation just as Lucretius weaves his words to illuminate the nature of things. 'Therefore I will begin to arouse and awaken [*pergam*] with my woven [*pertexere*] words' as 'I have unraveled' [*dissolui*] the 'mortal temple of the world' [*mundi mortalia templa*] (6.43–7), Lucretius says. He thus compares his weaving of words to a visionary [*docui*] drug that will wake the reader up from the darkness and show them the dissipative and dying warp and woof of nature's fabric.

Just like Triptolemus, Lucretius mounts his 'glorious chariot' to guide us on our journey. His sweet words disseminate the wisdom of materialism, just as Triptolemus distributed the seeds of Demeter. Triptolemus rode his serpent chariot across the ancient world to share the secret of

Figure 8.6 Triptolemus on a second-century Roman sarcophagus. Wikimedia Commons.

food security alongside the practice of the Mystery religion. The shared truth of the Mysteries and Lucretius' philosophy is that the world dissipates through iteration and iterates through dissipation like a vortex unravelling itself. A serpent draws the chariot of nature.

This is also the meaning of historical materialism. Lucretius is our epic charioteer on an increasingly dark journey from glorious Athens to Eleusis. There, we must go down into the sylvan-columned sanctum of the Telesterion. In the dark, we see the true light of things. Their nature is to flow and unravel towards death. We see a sensuous vision of ourselves as doors through which the universe passes as if we were a sieve or *calathus*.

But who is guiding Lucretius' chariot? He calls upon the Muse Calliope to 'show' [*praemonstra*] him the 'white limestone finishing line' [*candida calcis*] as he flows like a 'current' [*currenti*] along the road of truth. This is also an image of the road to Eleusis or the 'sacred way', which was paved with white stones and whose temple to Demeter was built into a limestone outcrop. It also invokes the early Greek philosopher-poet Parmenides' famous chariot ride along a sacred road of knowledge leading him from dark to light. We know that Parmenides was an initiate

Figure 8.7 Triptolemus and Korē, tondo of a red-figure Attic cup, c. 470–460 BCE, found in Vulci. Wikimedia Commons.

of the Eleusinian Mysteries and that his poem mirrors its initiation structure. The initiate travels to Eleusis, drinks the psychedelic *kykeon* in the dark temple,[11] and undergoes a journey led by the Eleusinan priestesses to meet the goddess who will give them the knowledge of nature they seek. Similarly, in Parmenides' poem, his chariot is led by maiden priestesses to the great goddess who gives him wisdom.

Calliope is not only the Muse of epic poetry invoked by Lucretius' heroes, Hesiod and Empedocles, but she was also known as the Muse of wisdom. Lucretius thus summons her as *callida Musa*, or 'Muse of craft, cunning, and wisdom through experience' (6.93). The guide or our guide is thus Calliope, the Muse of writing, wisdom, epic poetry, and mother of the celebrated Orpheus (son of Apollo). In Orpheus, we have

Figure 8.8 Cesare Dandini, *Calliope, muse of eloquence and epic poetry* (seventeenth century). Wikimedia Commons.

yet another iteration of the Eleusinian drama. The son of the mother loses his bride (Eurydice) while she is out in the forest, bitten by the spiralled snake. Orpheus makes a journey down to the underworld to recover her but is unsuccessful. The mythic reference here paints a dark picture of Lucretius' own guided journey to the dissipating end of the world. World history alternates between creation and destruction but ultimately tends towards dissipation. Orpheus, the poet of wisdom and oracular prophecy, returns empty-handed and is murdered by the turbulent attack of Dionysus' Maenads. Like all songs, the most beautiful ones must also come to an end. Nothing, even human wisdom, lasts forever. As Nietzsche, that great Epicurean, later wrote,

> Once upon a time, in some out of the way corner of that universe which is dispersed into numberless twinkling solar systems, there was a star upon which clever beasts invented knowing. That was the most arrogant and mendacious minute of 'world history', but nevertheless, it was only a minute. After nature had drawn a few breaths, the star cooled and congealed, and the clever beasts had to die. One might invent such a fable, and yet he still would not have adequately illustrated how miserable, how shadowy and transient, how aimless and arbitrary the human intellect looks within nature. There were eternities during which it did not exist. And when it is all over with the human intellect, nothing will have happened.[12]

Nietzsche understood the importance of planetary death as an anti-foundation for knowledge. Lucretius has something similar in mind when he invokes Calliope and not Venus as his guide for the rest of Book VI. Lucretius calls Calliope the 'repose of humans and pleasure of gods' [*requies hominum divomque voluptas*], echoing his invocation of Venus as *hominum divomque voluptas* (1.1–2). This time, however, Calliope is guiding Lucretius' chariot towards the unravelling of the world. Her wisdom and beautiful voice bring pleasure to the gods who desire and enjoy their dissipation. To humans, her wisdom brings a return [*re*] to a quiet and calm state [*requies*], as they, like the gods, desire their immanent dissipation along with the universe.

The context of the poet's summons of Calliope gives a new meaning to the *voluptas* invoked at the start of the poem. Desire is a material process that moves through gods, humans, and nature, but it is not only creative, as described in Book I. All desire tends towards dissipation. The gods are calm and wise enough to know this, but humans need the sirens' song.

Calliope was also one of the mothers of the sirens. Appropriately, the sirens were monsters, or 'showers of wonder', who offered to share all the wisdom of the world in their song for those travellers who would listen. However, those who stayed to listen were so enchanted that they would listen until they died. Beauty and wisdom are woven together with death and dissipation in the myth of the sirens. As the mother of Orpheus and the sirens, Calliope is also, therefore, a Muse of death. What better guide for Lucretius' descent to the underworld than Calliope?

Beauty is not static. It is only a metastable state sustained temporarily *through* dissipation and decay. The Mystery religion's original wisdom was that death comes again and again for the world. The temple of the world is woven and unwoven. Lucretius' important point is that tranquillity of mind [*requies*] does not come from mere philosophical contemplation but through art, beauty, and pleasure.

Conclusion

We need Calliope's tranquillity as the world unravels before us. The glory of Athens, with which Book VI begins, provides only a metastable eddy full of turbulence and natural disaster. As Lucretius says, this is because nature gives us everything in abundance, even death and destruction.

Disruption and turbulence are not exceptions to the rule but the rule itself. Therefore, we should not be surprised by turbulence but by the prevalence of stability. Since the world is mobile, fleeting, and flowing, negative impacts on human flourishing are part of the world. We must do our best to ride the tides together, but it certainly helps to know and accept the guiding process of dissipation. Now, let us follow our poet's lead in the next chapter as we begin our final descent into the core kinetic structure of this dissipation.

Notes

1   Robin Osborne, *Greece in the Making 1200–479 BC*, 2nd edn (London: Routledge, 2009).

2   For a detailed account, see Anne Baring and Jules Cashford, *The Myth of the Goddess: Evolution of an Image* (London: Arkana, 2000), 377–85. See also Gordon Wasson, Albert Hoffman, and Carl A. P. Ruck, *The Road to Eleusis: Unveiling the Secret of the Mysteries* (New York: Harcourt, 1978); and Carl A. P. Ruck, *Sacred Mushrooms of the Goddess: Secrets of Eleusis* (Berkeley, CA: Ronin, 2006)

3   Epicurus himself was said to have been initiated into the Mysteries according to Lucretius' contemporary Philodemus. Philodemus, *On Piety: Critical Text with Commentary*, ed. Dirk Obbink (Oxford: Oxford University Press, 1997), 20.554ff.

4   Peta Fowler, 'Lucretian Conclusions', in Monica Gale (ed.), *Lucretius* (Oxford: Oxford University Press, 2007), 211.

5   Carl Kerényi, *Eleusis: Archetypal Image of Mother and Daughter*, trans. Ralph Manheim (Princeton: Princeton University Press, 1991), 123.

6   William Shakespeare, *Romeo and Juliet*, ed. Burton Raffel (New Haven: Yale University Press, 2004), 2.6.9–11.

7   See Thomas Nail, *Lucretius II: An Ethics of Motion* (Edinburgh: Edinburgh University Press, 2020), ch. 4.

8   See Nail, *Lucretius II*, 101–4.

9   Karl Marx, *Economic and Philosophic Manuscripts of 1844*, trans. Rodney Livingstone and Gregor Benton (London: Penguin, 2007), 351.

10 See Thomas Nail, *Marx in Motion: A New Materialist Marxism* (Oxford: Oxford University Press, 2020), ch. 1.

11 Recent archaeological evidence confirms that the Mystery rites practised at Eleusis involved drinking psychedelically active ergot (the active fungus in LSD). The Greek Mysteries had been exported and reproduced with Greek sculptures and tools in Spain. For hard archaeochemical evidence of ritual ergot consumption, see Jordi Juan-Tresserras, 'La arqueología de las drogas en la Península Ibérica: una síntesis de las recientes investigaciones arqueobotánicas', *Complutum*, 11 (2000): 261–74. For evidence that these rituals were the same as those in Greece, see E. Pons et al., *Mas Castellar de Pontós (Alt Empordà). Un complex arqueològic d'època ibèrica (Excavacions 1990–1998)* (Girona: Museu d'Arqueologia de Catalunya, 2002), 481. For a popular description and analysis of these findings, see Brian Muraresku, *The Immortality Key: The Secret History of the Religion with No Name* (New York: St. Martin's Press, 2020).

12 Friedrich Nietzsche, 'On Truth and Lies in a Nonmoral Sense', in *Philosophy and Truth: Selections from Nietzsche's Notebooks of the Early 1870s*, ed. and trans. D. Breazeale (Atlantic Highlands, NJ: Humanities Press, 1979), 79.

9. As Above, So Below

Material history is the dissipation and spreading out of nature. However, this spreading out is neither evenly nor randomly distributed. Dissipation occurs through patterns of iteration and metastable states such as dendrites and vortices. These patterns are the language of history. As the universe unfolds, it traces out figures and patterns that it repeats across scales.

This chapter describes the existence and relationship between two significant patterns of material history as they appear in atmospheric and geological processes: dendritic dissipation and vortical iteration. Lucretius' intuition that nature is fluid and dynamic is fascinating and worth considering as a kinetic theory of history. Instead of a world of discrete things moving against a static or stable background of space and time, he describes a world of process, pattern, and metastable emergences. The earth, he says, makes itself through the process of destroying itself. It whirls itself into vortical hollows that increase the rate at which the whole process unravels itself, like water down a drain. We experience this as thunder, lightning, waterspouts, tornadoes, earthquakes, and volcanoes. They are also aspects of the fall and swerve of matter at the smallest levels.

Why is this so important in the scope of *De Rerum Natura*? Lucretius began by taking us on a gorgeous journey through the cosmos and back down to the smallest movements of dust motes scintillating in the sunlight. But what about everything in between? What of the movement of the earth? This section of the poem is crucial because it brings the macroscopic and the microscopic together and we see at last that the same dendritic and vortical patterns traverse every scale of nature. Now we can feel the full scope of nature as we are carried away on its swerving flows.

Waves of Thunder

The skies 'twist' [*turbine*] (6.126) like smoke, 'branch' [*silvam*] (135) like trees, and roll like waves [*fluctus*] (6.142). Thunder, according to Lucretius, is a shock wave of sound like the cracking sound produced by an awning 'stretched over great theaters' or 'drying clothes or flying papyrus sheets beaten by breezes' (6.110–15). Lucretius is correct that these different phenomena all produce sound waves through a similar physical process. They each involve increasing matter to the speed of sound. More specifically, increasing the pressure of matter rapidly produces a short-lived bubble of gas that collapses quickly and creates noise. In the case of thunder, this occurs through the scorching temperature of lightning on the surrounding cooler air. The rapid pressure and temperature increase create a hollow bubble that then pops and releases a large amount of energy. In the awning and papyrus, this happens through the whipping of the material. This poetic image does well to show the common kinetic pattern of dissolution in nature (thunder) and culture (clothing, papyrus, and theatre). Through the wind's dissipative power, matter is folded over itself and hollowed out into bubbles that swirl and pop into turbulent vortices.

Deafening sounds like thunder can also be created by tornadoes when 'a gathered blast of a strong wind has suddenly twisted itself into the clouds and, enclosed within, spinning and whirling more and more on all sides, forces the cloud to become hollow, its body thick all around' (6.124–7). Storm systems and tornadoes can increase their speed by forming a spiral or vortex. The vortex pattern lowers air pressure and allows wind to pass through the centre more efficiently. Increasing airspeed also increases the volume of sound and creates a deep rumbling noise like thunder or an earthquake. Like the 'cavitation bubble' produced by whipping cloth, hollow vortices are the most efficient pattern to dissipate a temperature or pressure gradient. Lucretius is right to identify vortical creation as a key to understanding dissipation dynamics. When large differentials of energy emerge, they often result in sudden and violent collapses.

This is the physical logic of bubbles. When we suddenly compress a bladder full of air, as Lucretius describes, it creates a cavitation bubble. A high-pressure wave moves dramatically out of the bladder and faster than the surrounding air. The world has all kinds of bubbles. But what is a bubble? It is an emergent form that sustains an energy differential.

For example, the inside of a soap bubble has a slightly higher pressure than the outside air. Nature, however, abhors a gradient, and so bubbles do not last forever. The bubble film dissipates, and higher energy states move to lower ones. The sudden collapse of a gradient creates an audible sound wave or 'pop'. In this way, the world is also a metastable bubble – the more massive and more sudden the gradient collapse, the more dramatic its wave. We can think here of the big bang.

Just as the ocean has waves, so does the sky, and, as we will see, so does the earth (6.142–4).

Sunt etiam fluctus per nubila, qui quasi murmur
dant in frangendo graviter; quod item fit in altis
fluminibus magnoque mari, cum frangitur aestus.

There are also waves among the clouds, which, so to speak, roar
loudly when they break. This likewise happens in deep
rivers and on the great sea, when the surging current breaks.

The world waves. But what is a wave? A wave occurs when a fluid starts to move faster on top than on the bottom. As a result, the top begins to curve around the base, generating a hollow vortex or bubble. An energy differential begins to build up in the wave, not unlike that of the bubble or the vortex. Eventually, the waveform becomes top-heavy. The tenuous metastable equilibrium breaks, and the higher energy state falls to a lower one. The wave breaks, and the sudden change in air pressure between the inside and outside produces a crashing sound.

History has waves, bubbles, and vortices. Energy builds up in little pockets and hollows and releases suddenly with a pop. The past does not disappear but is pulled along and folded up within the present like a curling wave. Things build on one another over long periods of relative metastability until, suddenly, they can no longer maintain their gradient, and violent changes erupt (revolutions, mass extinctions, cultural shifts). If the atmosphere, biosphere, geosphere, and oceans spread and swirl, why would history be any different? This the basis of Lucretius' naturalist theory of history.

Nature and history are *implex* (entangled) for Lucretius. Each natural pattern is an iteration of the others. Lucretius says that the clouds have 'waves' like the sea or rivers, they 'roar' like animals, and 'branch out' like trees (6.134–42). Oceans, rivers, clouds, trees, and animals all spread and branch out in dendritic patterns. The animal's veins look like the branches of trees, which look like waterways and veins of metal in rock.

Fiery Vortices

Inside clouds, a massive convection vortex is created as warm air rises from the earth, begins to cool, and falls back down. This process creates wind. Clouds are not entirely 'hollow', but they have central regions defined by contrasting temperature and pressure gradients (6.175–9).

> ventus ubi invasit nubem et versatus ibidem
> fecit ut ante cavam docui spissescere nubem,
> mobilitate sua fervescit; ut omnia motu
> percalefacta vides ardescere, plumbea vero
> glans etiam longo cursu volvenda liquescit,

When the wind has invaded a cloud, twisting around inside.
and has made, as I have shown before, the hollow cloud thicken,
it grows hot by its own speed, just as you see
everything become hot and glow by motion – why, a lead
projectile even melts as it spins on its long trajectory!

The speed of the wind inside clouds is also related to the generation of lightning. Storm clouds with lightning have much faster convection cycles and wind speeds than clouds that do not produce lightning. The faster the winds, the more they cause water droplets and ice crystals to rub against one another, 'just as if stone or iron strikes hard against stone, for then too light leaps out and fire scatters bright sparks' (6.163). Friction between water and ice creates an electric charge, just like walking on a carpet produces a static shock when you touch a metal doorknob. Inside the cloud, this creates a positive charge at the top and a negative charge at the bottom. As Lucretius describes, movement and energy tend to spread out, and lightning occurs where higher energies dissipate to lower ones. This happens most often through cloud to cloud lightning, which Lucretius designates as 'lightning'. When lightning strikes the ground Lucretius calls this a 'thunderbolt' [fulmen] (6.297).

> tum poteris magnas moles cognoscere eorum
> speluncasque velut saxis pendentibu' structas
> cernere, quas venti cum tempestate coorta

conplerunt, magno indignantur murmure clausi
nubibus, in caveisque ferarum more minantur;
nunc hinc nunc illinc fremitus per nubila mittunt,
quaerentesque viam circum versantur, et ignis
semina convolvunt e nubibus atque ita cogunt
multa, rotantque cavis flammam fornacibus intus,
donec divolsa fulserunt nube corusci.
Hac etiam fit uti de causa mobilis ille
devolet in terram liquidi color aureus ignis, (6.194–205)

Then you will be able to understand their great masses
and to observe their caverns built up as if from hanging
rocks, which when a storm arises and the winds fill
them out, closed in by the clouds they show their anger
with great rumblings and threaten like wild animals in their cages.
Now here, now there they emit growls
in the clouds, and seeking an exit they turn around and roll
the seeds of fire together from the clouds and so assemble
many and spin the fire within the hollow furnaces,
until the cloud is ripped apart and they gleam and flash with lightning.
It happens too from the following cause that this quick, golden
hue of liquid fire swoops down on the earth:

The clouds stack like rocks. They growl like animals and seek an exit
by turning and rolling like waves. The vortical structure of the clouds
is a furnace. Thunderbolts pour out like a liquid. Here again, Lucretius
shows us the *implex* or iterative nature of these dissipative patterns.
Mineral, animal, fluid, and technology are not separate ontological cat-
egories, but aspects or dimensions of the same process of dissipation.
Lucretius has taken poetic metaphor and made it literal. The effect is
startling.

The wild animals [*ferarum*] (6.198) of the clouds are turbulent like the
bacchant humans and animals which roamed the mountains in early
history. Wind and energy turn and whirl vortically in the clouds. They
dissipate suddenly in a thunderbolt of lightning that flows like liquid or
like a river down to earth.

Lightning bolts 'seek' the earth in a creative and experimental process,
using what are called 'stepped leaders'. The lightning 'tries out' various
paths to see which will be the most optimal. However, since conditions

are always changing, the 'optimal' lightning path is not predetermined. Lightning bolts flow down like a river watershed. Simultaneously, lightning moves upwards from the ground by the same process as that by which a tree branches out.

It is crucial here to take Lucretius seriously in his claim that lightning actively 'seeks, extends, sends out, puts forth, guides' [*mittunt*] (6.199) to meet another extension coming up from the ground. Without knowing the way in advance, the two seek each other step by step through experimentation. The history of nature and the nature of history proceed by a similar experimental technique, as we have seen.

Lightning bolts originate from the vortical convection hollows or caves inside storm clouds. Lucretius says that 'a vortex enters there and twists in the narrow space' [*insinuatus ibi vertex versatur in arto*] (6.277). Lucretius is correct to identify wind speed and friction as the source of energy in lightning bolts. His speculation that the source of fire also derives from the sun is only indirectly correct in the sense that the sun heats the earth, causing warmer air to rise. His poetic image of the 'ripening' [*maturum*] (6.282) of the thunderbolt is also quite lovely because it compares the organic growth of energy to the inorganic. Fruits ripen when energy collects in the hollow of the flower bud and lightning ripens when energy collects in the vortical convection hollow of the cloud. Both share a material pattern of motion. A lightning bolt 'occurs also when a force of wind from outside races and falls upon a cloud pregnant with a ripe [*gravidam maturo*] thunderbolt' (6.296).

Beneath the differences between organic and inorganic growth, there is a shared pattern of movement. The vortex is both creative and destructive at the same time. Energy seeks forms that help it spread out, to grow fruit, to make lightning bolts. This is not a pessimistic perspective, as some commentators have said about Book VI. Lucretius leads us down in a *katabasis* of transformation, where we must undergo the same dramatic unravelling as the universe. This is, after all, what the universe is doing.

History is a process of weaving and unweaving without a weaver. Everything weaves and is woven at the same time. A lightning bolt is a 'fiery vortex' [*igneus vertex*] that 'increases as it goes' [*volventia cursum*] and 'unweaves all the knots' [*dissoluent nodos*] that comprise 'entangled things held together through weaving' [*texta tenentur*] (6.297–351). The wind also 'weaves clouds together beneath the blue sky' [*subtexit caerula nimbis*] (6.482). So, the clouds are woven together but also generate lightning bolts that unweave them. Lightning spreads out its dendritic fingers like a weaver, like Penelope, to unweave what was woven.

In Book III, Lucretius described the soul as a metastable *disharmony* (3.98–105).[1] In Book VI, the earth and the cosmos are no different. Vortices emerge when 'dissimilar things must fight among themselves and cause turmoil when mixed' (6.369–70). Nature, like history, is in 'discord' and 'great tumult'. Material history is 'tossed about in turmoil' just like the appearance of lightning bolts when 'fluctuating periods of the year mingle cold and hot' (6.364).

Our poem began with the fertile mixtures of spring, and now those rich mixtures are vortically dissipating. The nature of 'things' entails a profound 'disharmony' [*discordia*] and 'turbulence' [*tumultu*] (6.366). From this turbulence come the metastable formations we call 'things'. Things come from a mingling of singular differences, like hot and cold air, which create the convection vortices that Lucretius describes. Just as the difference between rising warm air and falling cold air produces wind, all motion in nature occurs due to an imbalance or non-equilibrium state of disharmony. This is the basis of Lucretius' historical materialism. The more the energetic difference, the faster the motion.

When this 'vortex of wind on its own entangles itself in clouds' over water, it produces waterspouts. When it does so on land, it creates a tornado (6.423–50). Convection vortices of moisture (clouds) roam across the earth 'like hanging fleeces of wool' on sheep, emerging wherever differences mingle and become turbulent. Just as stars roam the universe, reducing energy gradients by feeding and dying, sheep roam the fields looking for water and grass, created by clouds that reduce gradients between hot and cold air.

Throughout Books V and VI, Lucretius unfolds the image of iterative dissipation across mineral, atmospheric, vegetal, and animal figures. This is not a projection of one thing on to another or a metaphor connecting separate things. Instead, Lucretius identifies a shared kinetic pattern that traverses all scales and forms of material organisation in nature. Humans, too, are whirling vortices dissipating energy into space. We roam around looking for gradients to collapse, just like storm systems, sheep, and star systems. Ice crystals in clouds 'grow', 'fruit', and 'branch out' as lightning seeks itself through stepped leaders.

Our Liquid Earth

Lucretius was perhaps the first to develop a fluid dynamic theory of geology. This is because, for Lucretius, there are no pure solids in nature. 'Geophilosophy' is, therefore, anti-foundational by definition. All solids and forms are only slow-moving fluids. So naturally, according to Lucretius, vortices and turbulence occur underground. The whole deep earth is in constant motion. It has eddies, convection cycles, and an entire shifting underground topology of 'rivers', 'lakes', and 'caves'. We live on a *mobile earth* [*terrai motibus*] (6.535).

'The earth [is] below, as it is above' (6.536–7). Patterns of dissipative iteration shape both sides. If wind is the movement that results from the shifting differential between hot and cold matter, we can say, as Lucretius does, that there are subterranean 'winds' [*ventosis*]. The earth's core heats magma, which then rises towards the surface. As it cools, it sinks back down towards the centre. This movement produces enormous convection patterns and vortices under the earth for the same reason that they occur in the atmosphere.

What Lucretius calls 'lakes' [*lacus*] are areas where metals and rocks gather together into underground pools or bubbles. Like lakes on the surface of the earth, underground 'lakes' can form, evaporate, and reform. The earth also has hollows or caves in the sense that there are pockets of gas trapped at various depths underground. The earth also has areas that are not entirely hollow but are at the centre of convection cycles.

Just as above ground, so below, 'the facts themselves require it to be everywhere similar to itself' (6.542). This is the bold and fascinating hypothesis we have been exploring in this chapter. Nature everywhere seems to follow similar patterns of organisation. These are not Platonic forms because they are in mortal, kinetic, and emergent features. They come into being for a while and then pass away. Their purpose is, after all, to facilitate the passing away of nature.

At this point, we might want to ask Lucretius how nature could have such common kinetic patterns if it is ultimately indeterminate. Why should habitual swerving give birth to emergent patterns of motion such as vortices and dendrites? Since Lucretius is not here to answer, let us venture a hypothesis.

If nature is habitually indeterminately swerving [*declinare solerent*], then it cannot remain static. Nature cannot, therefore, remain what it is. By swerving and unfolding, it must be differentiating itself without ever repeating. Process, as a process, is neither being nor nothing but an indeterminate differentiation and dissipation. Movement, therefore, entails mortality, becoming, and spreading out.

So, if all indeterminate movement, as a process, heads towards dissipation, then we will tend to find emergent patterns that are more efficient at dissipating energy than others, such as dendrites, waves, bubbles, meanders, and vortices. In other universes perhaps things would be so different that we would see different patterns. In this world, however, nature has experimentally invented the patterns Lucretius identifies as common in atmospheric and geological processes.

Earthquakes occur, Lucretius says, for reasons related to these patterns. Underground *bubbles* or caves can pop like an air-filled bladder and produce sinkholes on the earth's surface (6.545). The earth can also *meander* and 'creep in different directions' [*disserpunt*] (6.547) like a serpent [*serpunt*] and transmit these movements through *waves* in the earth as a wagon sends a shock when it hits a rock (6.550). The earth is like a vessel of water whose undulations sway the surface and create quakes (6.553–7).

> Fit quoque, ubi in magnas aquae vastasque lacunas
> gleba vetustate e terra provolvitur ingens,
> ut iactetur aquae fluctu quoque terra vacillans,
> ut vas interdum non quit constare, nisi umor
> destitit in dubio fluctu iactarier intus.

> It happens, too, when a huge mass is toppled by age
> from the earth into great and vast pools of water,
> that the earth also sways and is shaken by the water's undulations,
> just as at times a container is unable to be still unless
> the liquid within stops being rocked in unsteady undulations.

Magma flows create turbulence under the earth and ripple through the crust in seismic waves. Lucretius mentions that the taller humans build their towers, the more they sway in the seismic waves. Verticality and centralisation are not stable thermodynamic patterns in a turbulent world. Perhaps if human architecture employed natural patterns more, it would be more resistant to turbulence.

Inside the earth, matter 'twists all around' and gets 'aroused and stirred up', causing the earth to 'slip forward' and stop suddenly, threatening destruction (6.574). The movements of the earth pause to take a 'breath' before moving again. For Lucretius, the earth breathes like an animal and undulates like an ocean. It meanders like a snake and twists around like a storm. Nature is everywhere like itself. Earthquakes 'shiver and thus instill trembling' like the surface of the skin (6.593). The earth involuntarily shakes as Lucretius does in his moment of 'shivering' [*horror*] and ecstatic '*divina voluptas*' (3.28–30).

Lucretius says the earth has a kinetic agency. He says that the earth 'wishes' to eat itself by destroying cities (6.600). This is consistent with his more general theory of material desire described in Book II, in which all matter swerves and in swerving has 'will' [*voluntas*] (2.251–60).[2] The earth desires to consume itself no matter how 'imperishable' some people may think it is. When they experience an earthquake, they will remember that everything might be 'suddenly snatched from beneath our feet and carried into the abyss' (6.605–6).

This is history. Something external to the world does not cause the world. No hand of an unmoved mover or a benevolent god guides history. The accumulation of wealth, life, power, and prestige is a joke. Earthquakes remind us that the earth is in motion and, as such, will eventually take everything away. 'The summit of things may completely collapse and follow and that a jumbled wreck of a world may result' (6.606–7). This is the material logic of history. The taller and more complex the order, the less energetically stable it is. The summit is always less durable than the base, and so history traces the vortical and serpentine movement of the bottom to top and top to bottom. This is what we could call Lucretius' 'base materialism'.[3]

The Jaws of the Earth

If all things have pores [*foramina*], and if space [*inane*] and matter [*materies*] alternate with one another, then why would the earth itself be any different? When the pores and hollows formed by vortical and turbulent movements under the earth come to the surface, Lucretius says, we see volcanoes. The 'jaws' of the earth open up and let loose a 'swirling and turbulent blast' of smoke and fire.

There is no reason that the power of a volcano must come from anything supernatural. Again, nature is everywhere similar to itself, and the seeds of things are provided everywhere in abundance. Matter is an extraordinary shapeshifter and can create many things in many places. Look 'broadly and deeply at these matters and look carefully about at a distance in all directions' (6.647–8) Lucretius urges us. You will see similar kinetic patterns everywhere in nature. This is because material history iterates itself across scales and times as the multi-fractal structure of a tree iterates its branching pattern from its veins to its branches.

Just as disease 'meanders like a snake' [*serpens*] (6.660) through our bodies and we break out in fever, swelling, rashes, and limb pain [*membra dolorem*], so similar spreadings and disturbances can break out through the earth. Volcanoes are like swollen limbs or pustules heating up and changing shape. This image is a direct foreshadowing of the coming plague in Athens.

The meandering spiral pattern of the snake is a significant prehistoric figure of dissipative iteration. Things are created and destroyed but also tend to spread out and dissipate because the spiral is open without ever completely closing in on itself. There is no totality of things, only open processes. Disturbance in the form of disease, storms, and volcanoes has the same basic kinetic structure because history is material, liquid, and dissipative. There is disease and volcanism because we live in an open system ruled by indeterminate swerving.

Turbulence is not a fluke in nature, and Lucretius is not pessimistic in emphasising the centrality of dissipation. Commentators who see Book VI as defeatist or morbid have entirely missed the point. Life is not the meaning or end of the universe. The heart of Lucretius' ethics is that we should not fear death by fetishising life, yet that is precisely what these disappointed commentators are doing. The poet and his song will also dissipate into the cool. That, too, is part of poetry. Art is the process of joyful dissipation that makes it continuous with nature and not merely songs 'about' nature.

Volcanoes are not like bursting pustules of diseased skin any more than pustules are like volcanoes, or furnaces, or caves, or vortices of hot turbulent wind. There is no resemblance between things because there are no fully discrete things. Things are dimensions, aspects, iterations, or facets of nature, for Lucretius. Volcanoes carry on the motion of the universe by other means, 'and so it carries its heat far, far it spreads [*differt*] its ashes and rolls [*volvit*] out smoke with dense darkness' (6.690–1). Volcanoes spread out and roll, dissipate and iterate, fall and swerve, rain and pool. The atmosphere is just as much under the earth as it is in the sky. It is in the ocean, our bodies, and the cosmos because all matter is a mixture. This is the cosmic resonance we are supposed to grasp in these lines of Book VI.

Conclusion

For Lucretius, the causes of natural phenomena are open inquiries to be elaborated by further observation. Determining celestial causes is like trying to determine the cause of death of a body lying in the distance, the poet says (6.704–6). Here, Lucretius recasts philosophy as a kind of forensics or archaeology. This image needs some interrogation. Typically philosophy prides itself on 'first principles' and tries to determine the *a priori* forms, causes, and unchanging essences or laws of things. However, Lucretius completely inverts this Western assumption by focusing on the movement and processes of that which has *already happened*.

Our philosopher-poet arrives late on the scene of truth to find that it has already happened and is still underway. Lucretius scrambles to name all the possible causes without certainty or universality, hoping that one will be right. He experiments with possible theories and derives particular pleasure from the experimentation. That is, Lucretius finds that nature is fundamentally *historical*. So he does what history does. He experiments with various paths, all of which lead in their unique way to death and dissipation. Lucretius' materialism is a mortal philosophy without any metaphysical pretensions to universality. The dead body the poet finds lying on the ground is, in some sense, his own at the end of the world. There is only one general cause of death, and we are all undergoing it right now: dissipation. The question of materialist philosophy is one of forensic archaeology: what are the kinetic patterns that lead things to death?

Notes

1 See Thomas Nail, *Lucretius II: An Ethics of Motion* (Edinburgh: Edinburgh University Press, 2020), 68.

2 See Thomas Nail, *Lucretius I: An Ontology of Motion* (Edinburgh: Edinburgh University Press, 2018), ch. 10.

3 Georges Bataille, 'Base Materialism and Gnosticism', in *Visions of Excess: Selected Writings, 1927–1939*, ed. Allan Stoekl, trans. Allan Stoekl, Carl R. Lovitt, and Donald M. Leslie Jr. (Minneapolis: University of Minnesota Press, 1985), 45–52.

10. Of Poisons and Plagues

We come now to the final steps of our journey with Lucretius. Calliope has guided us to the underworld gates, which lie open before us and exhale their volcanic and oracular fumes. As we approach the truth, things get warmer and less stable. The path towards wisdom has not led us *beyond* the world to unchanging forms but deeper *into unravelling processes.*

For Lucretius, we do not find truth in any rational or philosophical doctrine, but in the dissipative material process of history itself. Philosophers and their theories will all die out like dirt devils in the sand. This is why the great sibyls of the ancient world took up residence at volcanic sites where the flows of matter continually weave and unweave things. Here they could glimpse a *vision* of nature. The turbulence and indeterminacy of the volcanic process is the truth of nature in the act. It reveals to us that history unravels the woven threads of the universe without balance, equilibrium, or harmony. History is both creative and destructive but tends towards dissolution. This is the most profound truth of every mystery and oracle in the ancient world: everything dissolves like the spiralling steam from a volcanic vent.

Upon first reading, Lucretius' paired discussion of 'strange fountains' and the plague at Athens may seem thrown together at the end of the book, but their connection is quite remarkable. Book VI began by connecting the turbulence of storms above the earth with the volcanism below. He argued that everywhere nature follows the same kinetic patterns of dissipation through vortical iteration. In the final leg of Book VI, Lucretius aims to show the same thing for the regions *between* the sky and ground, including volcanic springs and the biosphere, occupied by plants and animals.

This chapter aims to show that Lucretius' account of poisons and plagues in the final lines of Book VI has crucial implications for philosophy and our understanding of history. In particular, the movement of history defines the limits of all philosophy and human knowledge. History outstrips and outlives philosophy.

Ultimately, I conclude, history is the dissolution of the world without any ontological necessity of rebirth or divine redemption. However, this does not mean that the universe necessarily unravels into 'nothingness'. The final lines of *De Rerum Natura* are decisive regarding the complete unravelling of the world and the *indeterminacy* of any future world. We do not know and cannot know what will happen after the end of our world and the other worlds of the cosmos. All are born from the indeterminacy of the swerve and will be unravelled by it.

The Cumaean Sibyl

The first beautiful but haunting example of this process of material dissipation is the death of the birds that fly over Lake Avernus. The Romans believed that the lake was the entrance to the underworld, and that was why the birds died. 'Forgetting how to row their wings', Lucretius says, 'they lower their sails, droop with slackened neck, and plummet headlong [*praecipitesque cadunt*] to the earth' (6.743–4).

For Lucretius, however, the birds' death has nothing to do with the will of the gods. There are material explanations for the sudden death of birds or animals at certain places like this. These material explanations, though, do not repudiate the mythologies but rather bring out their truth. People see birds die while flying over Lake Avernus because 'This spot is near Cumae, where mountains are filled with acrid sulfur smoke . . . are well supplied with hot springs' (6.747–8). Nature supplies the earth with an abundance of processes that unweave and unravel all things. At some sites, we see this more than at others.

The kinetic images here are striking. The birds fall like the rain of matter [*praecipitesque cadunt*] down to the earth. Their bodies become soft and bendable [*molli*] like the plague victims (6.797; 6.1253; 6.1268). Birds and bodies fall like matter back to the earth to be unwoven. Like the fall of matter drawn to flow by its weight, the future of flesh is indeterminate.

The birds also 'forget' how to fly just as those infected by the plague forget who they are. Memory is a crucial feature that is unravelled by history. This is because memory is entirely material. It is woven and unwoven. Everything that might retain an observable trace of the past will eventually unravel at the end of the cosmos. Nature keeps all that it is and was, but only *indeterminately*. In other words, history itself is its own undoing. Like Penelope, it weaves the world to unweave it. No *sensible* trace is left. Yet the future will be related to what happened, although indeterminately so, due to the swerve. Therefore, we must distinguish between *historical materialism* that erases itself and falls like birds back into the volcanic lake, and the *materiality of history* that retains the past in a non-empirical and indeterminate sense.

Near Lake Avernus is the ancient town of Cumae, where the famous Cumaean Sibyl or oracle resided. Near Cumae also lie the tunnels at Baiae that lead to an underground river thought to be the river of the dead. It is no coincidence that this opening to the underworld is near a real material opening into the earth.[1] The Cumaean Sibyl was one of the oldest and most famous oracles of the ancient world, on a par with Dodona, Delphi, and Eleusis. After Lucretius, Virgil sang of 'Avernus with its rustling woods' and 'an inspired prophetess, who deep in a rocky cave sings the Fates and entrusts to leaves signs and symbols'.[2]

Oracular truth at these ancient sites does not come from a knowledge of a pre-ordained future but precisely the opposite. It comes from the

Figure 10.1 J. M. W. Turner, *Lake Avernus, Aeneas and the Cumaean Sybil* (1814 or 1815). Wikimedia Commons.

Figure 10.2 Michelangelo, *Cumaean Sibyl* (1511). Wikimedia Commons.

material process of indeterminacy and dissipation. The rustling woods at Avernus recall the speaking trees of Dodona. The priestess would listen to the singular sound of wind rushing through the trees and hear its meaning. The priestess at Cumae resided in her volcanic cave like the priestess at Delphi and interpreted the meaning of fallen leaves dropped by the wind.

It is hard not to see the resonance between this material performance and Lucretius' poetic materialism. The poet watches matter flow and fall indeterminately in various patterns on the earth and then guides the listener in 'unravelling' what happened. The leaves are like so many dead bodies seen from a distance. The poet-philosopher is like the detective-priestess who sees providence in the fall of the sparrow. This has nothing to do with fortune telling. Each fall is an iteration of the same truth: that history is its own indeterminate undoing.

This is what we might call the 'materiality of meaning'. Meaning, for Lucretius, does not reside in a human mental realm of linguistic forms. Meaning is nothing other than the immanent kinetic history of how things get distributed. It is the singular way that things came to be what they are. Meaning is not above and beyond or about things, but is rather the historical process of their ongoing relations. Meaning is historical.

When we say that something means something else, we are merely describing the *history* of relations of that something. In our lives, we often experience events that seem 'pregnant with meaning'. Yet we are not quite sure precisely 'what it all means'. That is because the event does not mean anything beyond its history of relational emergence, of which we are part. The history of relations connects with iterative patterns of what will happen next and, thus, the potential oracular character of any indeterminate process.

The indeterminacy of the process (falling leaves, for example) is related to the indeterminate future. So when the leaves fall, it is as if we are watching how history occurs and thus watching for patterns of how it may unfold in the future. Due to the indeterminacy of the conditions, this is always challenging; hence the need for the sibyl's wisdom.

This is why oracles occur at turbulent sites (volcanic vents, winds through sacred groves, and the babbling of springs). If the future is a process of dissipation and death in the last instance, then truth is fundamentally connected to chthonic processes. The earth unravels itself at these oracular sites.

Birds swerve through the skies but fall over Avernus. This is a poignant event for Lucretius. Birds are the historical source of human speech and song. They were some of the first poets of the earth, and Lucretius invokes them throughout his poem. The poet even identifies himself with the swooping and swerving of swallows (3.6). Now our avian poets swerve to their chthonic death. The flow of poison, like all flows, is indeterminate. We all live on a wing.

The Well of the Sacred Snake

Lucretius draws our attention next to the temple of Athena-Poseidon on the acropolis of Athens. Near the temple is a saltwater well where crows are said not to fly. For Lucretius, this is not because there is a goddess who is watching over the well, but because crows are not interested in drinking the salty water from it. The poetic image is even more fascinating.

Here again, Lucretius returns to a powerful image of the tree and the spring. However, instead of bringing life as they did throughout the poem, now they bring poison. These are material structures and patterns of motion at the heart of earthly existence and reveal the twofold nature of creation/destruction under discussion (6.749–50).

Figure 10.3 Cesare Nebbia, *The Contest Between Athena and Poseidon for the Possession of Athens* (1570s). Wikimedia Commons.

Est et Athenaeis in moenibus, arcis in ipso
vertice, Palladis ad templum Tritonidis almae,

There is also a spot within the walls of Athens, at the very vortex
of the citadel, near the temple of lifegiving Pallas Tritonis

The acropolis of Athens is at the very top [*vertice*] of the city, but the
Latin word *vertice* also means 'vortex', 'whirlpool', or 'eddy' (6.750). This
a powerful poetic image. The crown, peak, or summit of the city is also
a metastable vortex for increased dissipation. Athens is a vortex-serpent
city that gathers things together towards its centre to expand its mixture
and increase its dissipation of energy. This is precisely what makes it the
centre of the plague and death. The farmers from the countryside bring
the plague to the city centre. The citadel's vortex is both the peak of
the 'life-giving and nourishing' [*almae*] Athena/Poseidon and the place
where the earth opens up and releases its chthonic vapours.

The epithet *almae* invokes the opening epithet of *alma Venus* (1.2),
but this time the 'creative growth' of the gods is explicitly connected to
their role as chthonic dissipators. Athena is the mother of Athens who
spread grain but also a dark mother who bore the plague. It is that same
centripetal serpent that brought both. Since the plague came from the
countryside, the life-giving grain is twofold. It can be a bringer of life and
death: Athena/Poseidon, Demeter/Persephone.

Athens, from its beginning, expressed this twofold character. One day
Athena went to seek weapons from Hephaestus, the chthonic blacksmith
and god of volcanoes, and returned with a baby, Erichthonius. She
placed the baby in a box and asked the daughters of Athens' mythical
snake-king, Cecrops, not to open the box. When they opened it they saw
a baby with snake legs inside. Erichthonius, the earth-born or chthonic
one, became the second mythical king of Athens.[3] Homer describes him
as born of 'grain-giving Earth', and reared by Athena (*Iliad* 2.547–4).
This connects Athens again to Demeter and Triptolemus, the grain-son.
The snake was also a sacred animal of Athena, as it was for most goddesses historically. Lucretius thus invokes the snake's movement numerous times throughout Books V and VI to describe the motion of celestial,
volcanic, and plague bodies. The earth is everywhere like itself and the
spiral meander of the serpent.

At the temple well that Lucretius refers to, there was also a cult to
Poseidon-Erichthonius and Hephaestus. This was where Athena's snake

Figure 10.4 Paris Bordone, *Athena Scorning the Advances of Hephaestus* (1555).
Wikimedia Commons.

Figure 10.5 Peter Paul Rubens, *The Finding of Erichthonius* (between 1632 and
1633). Wikimedia Commons.

and the sacred olive tree resided as well.[4] Thus, the spring and tree are united in their dissipative movements by the iterative spiral meander of the snake.

What are poison and disease? They are processes of unweaving. Different things have different patterns woven by the first threads of matter [*dissimilem naturam dissimilisque texturas*] (6.775–6). Just as lightning 'unweaves the knots' of things, harsh smells, sounds, and textures can unweave things. Therefore, the volcanic and chthonic features of particular springs tend to unweave the lives of birds and other animals.

Delphic Laurels

Some trees are 'so noxious that they often bring about headaches' when you lie underneath them, Lucretius says. Lucretius does not give a specific reference here, but he may be thinking of tree pollen allergies. Earlier in the poem, bodies lay 'spread out' [*prostrati*] (2.29–33; 5.1392) under the trees by the river, rapt with pleasure. Now when bodies lie spread out in the grass [*prostratus in herbis*] (6.785), they might get headaches. This is far from a perfect or romantic vision of nature.

'There exists also in the lofty mountains of Helicon a tree accustomed to kill people with the horrible smell of its flower' (6.786–7). Again, Lucretius does not specify which flower he is talking about, but the image is striking. Helicon, the mountain of the Muses, was where Lucretius had wandered in search of new springs and new flowers to wear as a crown for his original poetic philosophy. He could have just as easily picked a flower that killed him. There is, therefore, a deep indeterminacy and contingency at the heart of philosophy and poetry. The flower's connection to the mountains and the Muses suggests that the location could be Delphi, where Apollo's famous laurel grew. Some scholars have convincingly argued that the laurels there were the neurotoxic oleander plant.[5] The flowers of oleander are toxic and could kill. Again, truth and death walk hand in hand. Volcanic fumes at Cumae, fungal ergot at Eleusis, and oleander at volcanic Delphi are all related to chthonic processes of dissolution and decomposition.

Noxious smells can cause people to 'fall down' and 'fall back', and can make 'drooping limbs slacken' [*languentia membra per artus solvunt*] (6.792–800). Even after eating a big meal and taking a bath it is possible for people to fall asleep and tumble down into the water [*ruinas*] (6.801). Just as the world will eventually 'fall into a confused ruin' [*mundi confusa ruina*] (6.607) and earthquakes 'threaten ruin' [*terra ruinas*] (6.572), so the sleepy bather expresses this fall into ruin in her own way. The microcosm is the enfolded or implicated macrocosm. Nature is everywhere like itself. Matter flows into all kinds of limbs that will fall, droop, and sink to their ruin. 'The noxious force and smell of charcoal' weaves and twists [*insinuatur*] its way like a serpent through our bodies, and fevers 'take hold of the limbs' (6.804).

So it is with various volcanic springs where noxious fumes undulate in waves [*aestus*] out from the earth. The birds flying above are hit by 'waves of vertigo' [*aestus*] and then 'fall by chance' [*cadat*]. When they hit the ground, life 'undulates' [*aestus*] out through their 'limbs' [*membra*], and they 'vomit' it out [*vomenda*]. It all happens in waves of turbulence (6.824–9).

The Libyan Sibyl and Dodona

Lucretius concludes his account of strange springs and lakes with the examples of the Ammon oracle or Libyan Sibyl and a well at the oracle of Dodona. The odd temperatures of both, according to Lucretius, are due to their proximity to 'seeds of fire', or what we would call volcanic or sulphurous hot springs (6.847–88). What is noteworthy, however, is the material relationship of both places to oracular wisdom. At the oracle of the Libyan Sibyl, the priestess would allow a boat to float around in the spring's turbulent waters. By this, she would speculate on future events. The future is related to indeterminacy, as are the chthonic flows. Just as the Roman goddess of chance, Fors Fortuna, was celebrated on a gambling boat floating on a river towards her temple, so the oracle is fundamentally related to the fluid indeterminacy of turbulent flows. These, in turn, are the material history of dissipation and death. More profound than the specific prognostications of the oracles is the material truth of their performance itself, which connects knowledge to death and indeterminacy.

At Dodona, oracles were also determined thermodynamically. The murmur of the fountain nearby spoke, as did the wind through the trees, the sound of doves, and the sounds of echoing bronze cauldrons.[6] Again, the point, for Lucretius, was not that a literal goddess spoke to the priestesses but that Dodona was connected to turbulent and chthonic flows whose movements were the performative truth of nature's dissipation.

Figure 10.6 Michelangelo, *Libyan Sibyl* (1511). Wikimedia Commons.

The Plague at Athens

Just as harmful vapours can rise from the earth through sacred springs in turbulent waves [*aestus*] to kill birds in the sky, so can deadly airs descend from the sky to kill humans and animals. 'The force of disease can suddenly arise and stir up [*conflare*] death-bearing destruction for the human race and herds of livestock' (6.1090–1). Death's turbulence comes from below and from above. Both airs follow the same falling, whirling, and dissipative kinetic pattern (6.1096–7).

ea cum casu sunt forte coorta
et perturbarunt caelum, fit morbidus aer.

When these happen by chance to have arisen
and caused the heavens to become turbulent, the air becomes diseased.

What is a plague? First of all, it is like all other turbulent processes in that its emergence is indeterminate [*forte*] and not entirely predictable. It is like a thunderstorm, tornado, earthquake, volcano, or hot spring. It is no coincidence that oracular interpretations also predicted the sudden rise of diseases. Oracles often interpreted diseases as punishments or omens of something worse yet to come. Lucretius, of course, rejects this kind of deterministic soothsaying while at the same time acknowledging the real material conditions of indeterminate emergence as a more profound truth about nature more broadly.

The emergence and spread of new diseases results from the general tendency of nature to experiment with new forms of dissipation and metastable iteration. Places where energy has become too heavily concentrated and accumulated, such as Athens, are sites ripe for energetic dissipation. Diseases rise and fall because they are spread out everywhere, according to Lucretius. However, they only become 'plagues' when a high concentration of energy (humans, plants, and animals) dies. Energetically speaking, every city is merely waiting for its next plague.

The plague is a form of turbulence [*perturbarunt*] that rapidly reduces an energy gradient between town and country. The higher the energetic difference between city and countryside, the more likely and devastating the plague. Lucretius explicitly compares the emergence of diseases with the appearance of clouds and storm clouds, saying that 'they often come together and rise from the earth itself'. Their development is 'untimely' [*intempestivis*] in the sense that it is as indeterminate as the habitual swerv-

Figure 10.7 Michiel Sweerts, *Plague in an Ancient City* (between c. 1652 and c. 1654). Wikimedia Commons.

ing of matter (6.110–11). Storms reduce a large energy gradient between hot and cold air just as plagues reduce gradients between large concentrations of certain kinds of life and smaller ones.

Turbulence develops at gradient transitions like spring and autumn, warm and cold. For example, Lucretius says, 'those who travel far from their home and fatherland are badly affected by the novelty of the climate and water because the conditions of life are so different' (6.1103–5). We know, of course, that different viruses and bacteria affect people differently based on their microbiome and their built-up immunities. Changing one's geographical climate requires a kind of gradient adjustment of one's organism to a new environment. This condition is ripe for turbulence and ailments. We might even hear echoes of Epicurus telling us that it is preferable to stay home and tend one's garden if possible.

When disease begins to spread, it 'sets itself in motion [*commovet*] and harmful air begins to creep about, it crawls slowly [*serpere*], like fog and clouds, and everywhere it goes, it perturbs [*conturbat*] and compels everything to change [*immutare*]' (6.1119–22). Lucretius was correct to note that infectious diseases spread in a non-linear pattern. They begin slowly but spread exponentially. More specifically, they spread out in serpentine branching patterns like lightning, and gather together spatially like clouds, more densely towards the centre and less densely at the periphery.[7] The plague at Athens may have started outside the city, but once it arrived in the city, the spread was like a dense fog tapering off into the countryside. The plague was like a storm system gathered from all over but settled in an area of urban density and high energetic contrast between rural and urban bodies. Then, like a storm, it used dissipation, in this case death, to reduce the difference between urban and rural population density. It disturbed and changed everything from a higher to a lower energy state.

The 'death-bearing wave' [*mortifer aestus*] hits us and absorbs our bodies, transforming and unravelling them. The high-energy density of urban life is literally 'drained' [*exhausit*] out into the streets and back into the earth like a heavy rainstorm. The disease travelled the pathways and roads branching in and out around Athens and devastated them [*vastavitque*] (6.1140).

The Plague Body

The plague body is a microcosm of broader atmospheric and volcanic processes of turbulence. Everywhere nature unravels itself by the same kinetic patterns of dissipation. Just as the skies fill with fiery lightning in a thunderstorm and the earth fills with fire during volcanoes, the plague has human 'heads on fire with fever and their two eyes reddening with light welling up beneath' (6.1145–6). Just as hollow vortical pockets of pressure emerge in the skies and underground, they also emerge as ulcers on the body. The plague closed up people's throats, and they 'poured out blood' from their tongue like rain from the clouds. Their 'blackened throats' were like the dark storm clouds or the chthonic earth. The poetic member, the tongue, 'the interpreter of the mind', can now only dissipate itself in blood.

This is a gruesome but significant event. The material basis of human speech, poetry, and philosophy is, and always has been, in the body, as a member or limb [*membra*] of the world. The human body is a limb of the world that, like all other limbs, can swell, bleed, and break down. When it does, poetry is impossible, and philosophy unthinkable. In other words, philosophical poetry is profoundly material, historical, and finite. There is nothing even remotely universal about what we typically call truth, knowledge, or beauty. The turbulent tides of history will not only wash all of it away but will change the world such that our understanding of it is always out of date.

To say that such an idea is pessimistic or gloomy assumes that universal knowledge was possible in the first place. This is an error. History takes every opportunity to correct this misunderstanding. There is nothing especially sad about the fact that human knowledge occurs in our material bodies and that one day all those bodies will break down. Our knowledge will not pass on to others. No one will tell human history, and all traces of human intelligence will be eradicated.

For Lucretius, the same is true of everything in all worlds. We are not unique in our dissipation. It is precisely the material process of our dying and dissipating that is the performative truth of nature. The truth of philosophical poetry is not in its content but its performative action, its dissipation. The plague demonstrates this dramatically by slowly degrading the body limb by limb. Philosophy and poetry will not save or redeem us from this. There are no peaceful Epicurean gods for us to contemplate. Our ideas of the gods will die with our bodies. The tongue will pour out blood, and the mind will unravel and forget itself.

The final section of our poem is a profound meditation on death, but not in an *existential* or *intellectual* sense. Lucretius, as usual, is interested in the *material process* of dying. He wants to show us a vision of an *intimate bodily* dissipation that connects us physically to nature. To wish that you were outside this dissipation is to wish you were not what you are: nature. Can we witness and accept death as nature? The desire for immortality is a profound hatred of matter and motion (hylephobia/kinophobia).[8]

Nature habitually swerves indeterminately, and that includes us. The swerve is not just the source of our relative freedom but also of our dissipation and illness. Our desires and sufferings are the two 'sides' of the same single-sided Möbius strip. The plague may be painful and sad, and we do not have to like it. Poetry, philosophy, and even medicine cannot help us. That is the point. In a world of material flows and processes, there is no way out. No gods, immaterial minds, or immortal souls can save us from pain and dissipation.

Of course, we should avoid pain, suffering, plague, and death as far as we can, but there is no guarantee of absolute security. Is death the meaningless negative of life, or is it that there is material truth in our suffering and decay? Are we bold enough to affirm both without fear and resentment? Can we drink the draught of materialism stripped of all pretensions to universality, humanism, and absolute knowledge?

Instead of poetry, the plague body breathes out the reek of rotting corpses and vomits out filth like the noxious fumes of sulphur springs. Instead of the graceful stroll through the mountains of the Muses, the limbs of the plague body 'convulse' [*membra coactans*] and are 'unwoven' [*dissoluebat*] (6.1161–2). Instead of calm pleasures, 'the rational faculty of the mind was perturbed by grief and fear, the brow was gloomy, the facial expression frenzied and wild' (6.1183–4). Since nature interweaves body and mind, disease destroys all our usual tools for reducing suffering and creating pleasures. By dehumanising the human, the plague slowly destroys all the material conditions for our salvation or redemption.

Into the Cool

The inside of the plague body becomes a 'furnace' like Mt Etna (6.681). Lucretius says that the victims' bodies became so hot that 'Many fell headlong from on high into well water, hitting the surface with their mouths wide open' (6.1178, 1174). This is such a haunting image of history. History is the 'fall' of the universe into the cold darkness of space. The big bang formed an enormous inner fever so hot that, to cool itself, it had to spread out extremely fast, and is still spreading. We are all, alongside the universe, falling face first, mouth open, into the dark. Just as the plague branches out to reduce an energetic gradient from high to low, the plague body seeks to reduce its inner heat so rapidly that it dies by cooling. In this brutal example, the well becomes a literal gateway to the chthonic underworld of death.

The birds and beasts, who did not die, fled to the cold forests. 'Scarcely at all in those days could any bird be found' (6.1219–20). The messenger of speech, music, poetry, and oracle, the bird, fled to the dark forests. Domesticated animals, however, had bound their fates to humans and died quickly.

The Return of the Swerve

The plague, like nature, is an indeterminate process. Who will survive and who will die? After the world destroys itself, will something else emerge? What cures one person kills another. Like history, the plague is a process of mutation that 'changes everything', including itself. It experiments just as the plague doctors experimented with cures.

This is a critical insight into the nature of materialist knowledge and history. There are no universals, no panaceas, only trials and tests taken one step at a time. Knowledge and beauty are not immune to this process. They experiment with different iterative orders of dissipation, step by step, without immortality or final cure. Philosophy and poetry are akin to medicine and the *pharmakon* in Lucretius' ultimate plague city.

The honeyed cup of wormwood is not only a metaphorical image (1.936). Philosophical poetry works *on* and *through* the body. Eating herbs can be just as mind-altering and beautiful as philosophical poetry. Drugs and ideas work at the same immanent level in unique ways. The action of their *pharmakon* is equally material, sensuous, and just as experimental. Just as we tend to think of practical skills or culinary recipes as non-universal knowledge, so it is with philosophical poetry, for Lucretius. It is all about the effects that performance can circulate. The form of materialist knowledge does not lie in the propositional statement 'everything flows' [*omnia migrant*] (5.830), but in the changing performance of the unique *being that flows* or flows by uttering the words 'everything flows'.

Lucretius writes that 'Nor was there a sure method of cure that worked for all' [*nec . . . certa*] (6.1226), recalling the *incerto tempore, incertisque loci* (2.218–19) of the swerve. Therefore, the plague is an expression of radical indeterminacy, which does not necessarily lead to absolute nothingness or rebirth. It is neither optimism nor pessimism. This is the idea that Lucretius wanted to leave us with in this final section on the plague: responsiveness to indeterminacy. Of the victims who take the same medicine, some 'gaze upon the temple of the sky' [*caeli templa*] while others 'flow down the path of death to the river of oblivion' [*exitio letumque*] (6.1228–9). For Lucretius, the appropriate way to handle this indeterminacy is to accept what is out of our control as part of a more extensive dissipative process, which is not separate from ourselves. The worst way, however, would be to hate the world of matter and kill yourself from fear of death because you could not control it. Better to die trying to survive than to kill for unnecessary luxury.

Here is where Lucretian ethics can offer amelioration for some. We should avoid the fear of death because it leads to all kinds of unethical behaviour (greed, pride, murder, accumulation, and even suicide).[9] Why add these nasty behaviours on top of our lot of natural suffering? Furthermore, as long as the body is capable of pleasure, there is no point in mental anguish. It is pointless to die of anxiety over one's death when such an end is not immediately pending (6.1230–4).

Some died from drinking too much water from the Silenus water fountain. Here also, Lucretius recommends a diversity of non-destructive pleasures. Drink until no longer thirsty. Here we see what happens when unchecked accumulation runs wild. This is what happened to Silenus, an old companion to Dionysus, who drank too much from a fountain. He fell asleep and was captured by King Midas, who made Silenus share his oracular wisdom: 'the best thing for a man is not to be born, and if already born, to die as soon as possible'.[10] In other words, the existence of man as an isolated individual separate from nature is an error. The best thing for a creature who thinks this way is to return to death and avoid a world that they will feel is full of suffering against their 'life'. Living is a very brief affair, but dying will go on for billions of years. Another way to interpret Silenus' wisdom is that the best way to live is *through dying* – like the death of the universe. The faster we die could also mean the more rapidly we increase the energetic dissipation of the universe.[11] How can we live such that we let life pass through us like water through the woven *calathus*?

We can interpret this 'death' in line with the *katabasis* of the Mysteries or as the energetic dissipation of bodies. How can we live by letting ourselves die and not trying to hold what we cannot? The flow of the Silenus fountain, for example, cannot be possessed or accumulated.

The Death of Religion

The plague exposes the woven finitude of the world. In the plague, we see intimately and sensuously the base materiality of things. The plague reveals all idealisms and spiritualisms as profane material habits, nothing but habits. The gods do not come to the rescue. They do not relieve the intense physical suffering of the body. The plague diminishes and deranges the body so severely that the sick cannot observe religious rites, nor do they feel that such reverence has any worth. 'Death filled up all the holy shrines of the gods with lifeless bodies . . . Nor indeed any longer was reverence of the gods or their divinity of much worth' (6.1272–7).

The plague is terrible, but the sheer drama and suffering of the event also tell us something about the nature of things. The plague tells us that matter is woven and unwoven by the same stroke. It tells us that all will perish because all is material. Not religion, philosophy, science, or the arts will stop the terror or outlive the death of humans or the world. 'All that is solid melts into air, all that is holy is profaned, and man is at last compelled to face with sober senses his real conditions of life, and his relations with his kind.'[12] Marx wrote these words about that other great murderous plague descended upon the world: capitalism. The causes of each are different, but the event of abject suffering and violence is no less spectacular and summons similar attention to the *real conditions of life*.

Conclusion: Anti-Venus

The poem's final lines leave us with two images of history: *indeterminacy* [*subita*] and *turbulence* [*perturbatus*]. The drama of the plague provides us with an intimate vision of the indeterminate nature of things without any metaphysical guarantees or solid foundations for immortality, knowledge, or beauty. Turbulence creates metastable orders but also unstable orders. Our mistake is to expect to be able to control them or know them entirely, and to fear what we cannot prevent: death.

Nature dissolves itself and human culture. Nothing is immune to the flow of matter. The population of Athens became turbulent when the sudden event of plague broke out and led to the collapse of basic social decency. The last lines of the poem describe families burning their dead on other families' funeral pyres and then violently attacking one another. If anything, this is a strongly anti-progress narrative. However, the point is not that things cannot 'get better', relatively speaking, but that in the long run, the terms of progress and regress are not universal or absolute. Everything unravels. The only universal is the continual transformation and destruction of the universe.

The plague is a fitting end to our poem because it describes the same indeterminacy (dissipation) and turbulence (iteration) of the birth of Venus, but from the other side.

The plague, like Venus, dominates air, sea and earth (6.1139–4; 1.2–4); it is brought by the wind (6.1138), which flees Venus (1.6); it empties the lands (6.1139), which Venus fills with life (1.2–5); its *mortifer aestus* makes the fields deathly (6.1138), while Venus releases the *genitabilis aura favoni* (1.11) and makes the land fruitful (1.3, 14, 18); the plague kills the birds and beasts (6.1216–24), which Venus causes to propagate (1.12–20); it heaps up the dead *catervatim* (6.1144), while Venus causes propagation *generatim* (1.20); it fills men's hearts with despair (6.1152, 1233), where Venus fills animals' hearts with desire (1.19).[13]

Lucretius structured his poem along Empedoclean lines. It begins with love and life and ends with strife and death. Each, as Empedocles wrote, was twofold and inseparable. However, unlike Empedocles, Lucretius does not grant any necessity of rebirth at the end of the world. Love and strife are twofold but are also, for Lucretius, *indeterminately* related such that one *may* come out of the other, but when and where is not knowable or guaranteed. Hence, *De Rerum Natura* does not end with rebirth.

Notes

1   Mike Dash, 'The Unsolved Mystery of the Tunnels at Baiae', *Smithsonian Magazine*, 1 October 2012, https://www.smithsonianmag.com/history/the-unsolved-mystery-of-the-tunnels-at-baiae-56267963/ (accessed 12 July 2021).

2   Virgil, *Eclogues, Georgics, Aeneid I–VI*, trans. H. Rushton Fairclough and G. P. Goold (Cambridge, MA: Harvard University Press, 1999), Book 1, ll. 376–9.

3   See Ovid, *Metamorphoses: Volume I (Books 1–8)*, trans. Frank J. Miller, ed. G. P. Goold (Cambridge, MA: Harvard University Press, 1916), 2.552–65 for a fuller version.

4   Jeffrey M. Hurwit, *The Athenian Acropolis: History, Mythology, and Archaeology from the Neolithic Era to the Present* (Cambridge: Cambridge University Press, 1999), 32.

5   Haralampos V. Harissis, 'A Bittersweet Story: The True Nature of the Laurel of the Oracle of Delphi', *Perspect Biol Med*, 57.3 (2014): 351–60.

6   Diego Chapinal, 'Oracles and Sound: Their Importance at the Sanctuary of Dodona', in Linda C. Eneix (ed.), *Archaeoacoustics II: The Archaeology of Sound – Publication of the 2015 Conference in Istanbul* (Myakka City, FL: OTS Foundation, 2016), 25–32.

7   Nick Evershed and Andy Ball, 'How Coronavirus Can Spread Through a Population and How We Can Beat It', *The Guardian*, 22 April 2020, https://www.theguardian.com/world/datablog/ng-interactive/2020/apr/22/see-how-coronavirus-can-spread-through-a-population-and-how-countries-flatten-the-curve (accessed 20 August 2020).

8 See Thomas Nail, *Lucretius II: An Ethics of Motion* (Edinburgh: Edinburgh University Press, 2020), ch. 2.

9 See Nail, *Lucretius II*, ch. 2.

10 Plutarch, *Morals*, trans. Arthur R. Shilleto (London: George Bell and Sons, 1898), 66–88.

11 For a longer description of some activities that would increase our planetary dissipation, see Thomas Nail, *Theory of the Earth* (Palo Alto, CA: Stanford University Press, forthcoming), ch. 14.

12 Karl Marx and Friedrich Engels, *The Communist Manifesto*, trans. Samuel Moore (London: Penguin, 2002), 223.

13 See Monica Gale, *Myth and Poetry in Lucretius* (Cambridge: Cambridge University Press, 1994), 226.

Conclusion: Unmaking History

Is this the end of Book VI, of *De Rerum Natura*, of the world? It's indeterminate. It's up in the air. Many readers have felt dissatisfied with the ending of the poem. Some commentators have even argued that the poem is unfinished and incomplete because it ends with the plague at Athens. However, my feeling is that this reaction says more about the reader's expectations than about the poem itself. Rather than speculate about alternative endings to the poem, I would like to suggest an interpretation that makes sense of it differently.

If we assume that Lucretius was an Epicurean, then we should certainly be upset and confused by the conclusion of *De Rerum Natura*. The proper Epicurean conclusion to an 'atomic epic' ought to be the contemplation of peaceful, unchanging gods unaffected by the world's death because they live in the everlasting calm between worlds. Furthermore, our tranquil Epicurean minds should help us prevail in the face of suffering and death more than Lucretius' description of the plague suggests. After all, what is the point of using reason or thinking of the gods if nature can just indeterminately swerve into a state of turbulence that destroys our minds, our bodies, ethics, and the gods themselves?

Lucretius offers a profoundly indeterminate ending to the poem and the end of the world in which no static gods live in between worlds. They are just ideas in our minds. No gods, ideas, or arts can save us from suffering or the end of the world. Furthermore, for Lucretius, the swerve is an ongoing aspect of all material reality. This means that matter is fundamentally unpredictable and not under our physical or mental mastery. The world, including our bodies and minds, may swerve and become so turbulent that we cannot mitigate it with truth or beauty. Lucretius and Epicurus agree that there is no reason to fear what happens after death. However, for Lucretius, for whom the swerve is a much more significant and widespread aspect of nature, we still must confront the painful material process of being unwoven strand by strand.

Is this pessimism? I think not. For Lucretius, indeterminate dissipation through movement is the most fundamental feature of our world. It is not a question of optimism or pessimism but of the *nature* of things to course and flow.

All creations are iterations and patterns towards dissipation, but the birth of new worlds from the unravelled strands of the old ones is not a necessity. It is an indeterminate event. Accordingly, the poem ends with turbulence and indeterminacy. To conclude *De Rerum Natura* with happy thoughts of static gods would be absolutely anathema to the poem.

The Ends of Things

There are several good reasons to think that the plague at Athens was the intended ending of the poem. First, the end of Book VI is similar to the conclusions of all the other books. Book VI contains 1,286 lines, which is approximately the same length as the other five books. Also, all six books open with themes of creation and end with descriptions of dissipation or death.[1]

Second, beginning the book with love and life and ending it with strife and death follows perfectly Lucretius' central poetic influence, Empedocles. According to Empedocles, the universe begins with love and spreads out to finish with strife. Then it returns to love, and so on indefinitely, back and forth. Ending with death is also an appropriate fit for the themes of the Mystery religions that Lucretius invokes in Books V and VI. Lucretius creates an image of himself as our guide on a path. Calliope, the Muse of wisdom and death, leads him down to the destruction of the earth and the cosmos. The initiates of Eleusis, for example, were led on an arduous path to the entrance of the underworld. What they saw there was ineffable and beyond word or description. Our poet-guide can take us down and show us the full material unravelling of the plague body. He can hand us the *kykeon*, but he cannot say what we will see. The language of vision pervades the entire poem, but at the end of the road to Eleusis, we are left in the dark to see a unique vision.

Third, Book VI opens with a discussion of Athens as the mother of grain dissemination and ends with the destruction of Athens, its grain, and its people. If the poem is unfinished, why does it end in a perfect compositional ring?

Fourth, every topic the poet said he would discuss in his brief resume of Book VI he has covered by the end of the book.

Fifth, Lucretius explicitly refers to Book VI as his final goal (6.92).

Some interpretations, however, do not fit well with the plague at the end of the book. For example, the great twentieth-century French philosopher, and interpreter of Lucretius, Gilles Deleuze could not believe that *De Rerum Natura* could end with the plague. He wrote that

> I fantasize about writing a memorandum to the Academy of the Moral Sciences to show that Lucretius' book cannot end with the description of the plague, and that it is an invention, a falsification of the Christians who wanted to show that a maleficent thinker must end in terror and anguish.[2]

Deleuze is upset with the conclusion because he had developed a vitalist interpretation of the swerve as a 'creative force' or *conatus*.[3] So Deleuze would rather publicly propose conspiracy theories about the text's falsification than admit that his vitalist interpretation of Lucretius does not fit with the book. Deleuze could not face the challenging Lucretian conclusion that, at the end of the universe, there is no vitalist redemption, no necessity of cosmic rebirth. There is no salvation, just an indeterminate swerve.

Ryan Johnson is right to note that

> in a way, this means that Deleuze thinks that Lucretius is not Spinozist enough. While Deleuze sees Spinoza's 'incredible book five' of his Ethics as an extraordinary thinking at infinite speeds that ends in the joyful affirmation of the world, *De rerum natura* strangely concludes a book of immanence and pleasure with a gruesome picture of death and destruction.[4]

If we think of Lucretius only as a philosopher of pleasure, affirmation, and life, then the ending seems 'strange'. But if Lucretius is a philosopher of indeterminacy, dissipation, and iteration, then the end of the book is perfect.[5]

However, it is also important to note that the book's ending is not a summary of the poem. This fact also befits a book in which dissipation, motion, and history are primary. There is no synthesis or summary of the world. The world spreads out and unravels without syntheses. Matter flows out until the world is gone.

Lucretius' universe is not a harmonious place of equilibrium where destruction *always* balances creation. Ontology is profoundly historical and asymmetrical because matter flows. Flow necessarily entails global dissipation and dissolution from higher energy to lower energy. The swerve is indeterminate, not random, because matter always responds to what happened before. As such, what comes after is always slightly more spread out (globally speaking) than before. This is entropy. The world ends in death and dissipation.

Lucretius was, therefore, much closer to contemporary understandings of physics than Spinoza was. Lucretius was correct that the sun will burn out and that the earth, and all the planets, will eventually dissipate all their energy into space. With more recent knowledge of black holes, cosmologists mostly agree that supermassive black holes will eventually absorb all matter in the universe and then absorb one another. Over time everything in the universe will be broken down into quantum fluctuations of energy. After that, no one knows what will happen.

The universe may stay in this more or less scattered state of quantum flux for an incredibly long time. It is also physically possible that the vacuum fluctuations of energy may generate enough gravity to start pulling everything back together. Or more dramatically, it is also consistent with the standard model of particle physics that quantum fluctuations might suddenly alter the fundamental laws of the universe and create an entirely new universe with new laws. This is what physicists call 'vacuum decay'.

Of course, Lucretius does not discuss these possibilities, but at least his philosophy is not incompatible with them. Lucretius' notion of indeterminacy (the swerve) and the existence of many worlds is entirely consistent with the known laws of quantum physics.

Concluding Thoughts on History

What does all of this tell us about the nature of history and the history of nature? It tells us that history is *made* through the process of *unmaking*. Lucretius gives us a philosophy in which history is fundamental. He does not assume that there are pre-existing forms, essences, or substances that move on a fixed background of space and time. Instead, he submits every single thing in his philosophy to the condition of a mobile process defined by the principles of indeterminate dissipation and iteration.

This is a radical position. It means that even the *nature* of things itself is fundamentally *historical*. This is perhaps the first truly 'historical ontology' in the West. What then is the *nature* of things, given the primacy of historical movement? For Lucretius, it must remain an open and indeterminate question because nature itself is indeterminate. As Lucretius does, we can still venture descriptions of the tendencies that we see, but the problem cannot receive a final answer forever and for all time. It can only receive a historical solution, which changes the conditions of the problem.

History, then, is just the experimental tendency of nature to spread itself out until it dies. Along the way, it indeterminately creates many worlds with potentially different laws of nature. In the end, nature may indeterminately swerve and recreate itself or not.

This book ends, therefore, as Lucretius ended his: with frayed threads dangling into an uncertain future.

Notes

1 'All six books of the DRN (with the possible exception of book 5) end in darkness, with death and decay and human folly.' Monica Gale, *Myth and Poetry in Lucretius* (Cambridge: Cambridge University Press, 1994), 228. Book V ends with a discussion of luxury and the arts, but immediately before that is a longer discussion of war.

2 Gilles Deleuze and Claire Parnet, *Dialogues*, trans. Hugh Tomlinson and Barbara Habberjam (New York: Columbia University Press, 1977), 15.

3 Gilles Deleuze, 'Appendix I: The Simulacrum and Ancient Philosophy: 2. Lucretius and the Simulacrum', in *The Logic of Sense*, ed. Constantin V. Boundas, trans. Mark Lester and Charles Stivale (New York: Columbia University Press, 1990), 266–79.

4 Ryan J. Johnson, *The Deleuze–Lucretius Encounter* (Edinburgh: Edinburgh University Press, 2017), 14.

5 The difference between Spinoza and Lucretius is also important as a historical reference point for the new materialisms. For those, like Jane Bennett and Elizabeth Grosz, who trace their lineage to Spinoza, a similar vitalism results. Lucretius offers a different starting point.

Afterword

It is bittersweet to have completed this eight-year project on Lucretius. I can honestly say it has guided and changed my thinking on almost every issue in philosophy. I would like to conclude with some final reflections on the project as a whole.

What have I learned from all this? For starters, I have a new-found appreciation of the deeply philosophical nature of mythology. Lucretius weaves myth and philosophy together so beautifully and compellingly. None of my education in philosophy quite prepared me to treat mythology as having such philosophical significance. Philosophers often read myth as pre-philosophical and 'irrational'. This has unfortunately influenced how Lucretius, the Greek poets, and many Indigenous thinkers have been received by European and American philosophers. Lucretius has been my introduction to the critical world of mythology as philosophy.

Teaching and writing about mythology has also been fun and compelling. I have watched my students' attention pick up dramatically when I start telling the myths. There is something primal and compelling about storytelling that is attenuated in proposition-based philosophy. I feel now the power and continuity of storytelling with philosophy in ways I had not before.

I also was surprised to have learned of so many differences between Lucretius and Epicurus. I did not set out to show how different the two were, and yet the more I was forced to tangle with the presence of 'the master' in *De Rerum Natura*, the more it struck me how original a thinker Lucretius was. His style is subtle and satirical. Lucretius is a trickster who never bores.

When I began, I assumed that there were atoms in Lucretius, that he believed in the gods, that he used the swerve in the same way Epicurus did, and that his ethics were identical to those of Epicurus. Along the way, I discovered how textually unsupported each of those assumptions was. I doubt these findings will please most Epicureans, since most rely on *De Rerum Natura* as a key text for their understanding of Epicurus. The two share much, but they disagree on several core ideas that we should not ignore. Lucretius likely learned of the swerve from Epicurus, but he made it much more integral to his philosophy than Epicurus did. Lucretius was not a rationalist. We owe our understanding of the swerve to him and not to Epicurus. Among other things, I hope to have sown a few seeds of doubt upon the oft-repeated story of 'Lucretius the Epicurean fundamentalist'.

Relatedly, I have a learned a new appreciation for the critical role that performance plays in knowledge. Lucretius was heir not only to the poetic tradition but to the oracular, ecstatic, epiphanic, and Mystery traditions that inspired ancient poets for thousands of years. Classical philosophy and science have tried to distance themselves from these older mythopoetic traditions. In doing so, we have lost something important that Lucretius wanted to recover at the close of antiquity. In my view, Lucretius shows us that we need not impose divisions between science and poetry, philosophy and mythology.

Lucretius has inspired in me the need to rethink the performative aspects common to both the mythopoetic tradition and the modern epistemological one. I see now that there is a material and performative truth to the epiphanic and the Mystery traditions that has been caricatured by scientific rationalism in the name of 'moving beyond' it. Many 'witches' and Indigenous peoples have been murdered for their mysteries so that Europeans could affirm the superiority of reason and immateriality.

Reading Lucretius has also had an effect on me as a thinker and writer. I am now much more interested in studying the material, aesthetic, and ecological aspects of knowledge. Several of my readers have remarked how playful and creative my writing is in these books compared to my others. Working with poetry and myth have provoked in me a style and tone that has felt more exploratory and colourful. I hope I can find this voice in future works.

I also credit Lucretius for the key insight that the nature of movement is *indeterminate*. In my view, the swerve is one of the most important concepts in the history of thought. This view finds evidence in certain interpretations of quantum physics, but Lucretius has helped me think through many of its implications that physics has not. Lucretius has walked me through many philosophical problems that I might not have tried to tarry with on my own. He has also drawn me to many images of thought like the vortex and the woven basket that now circulate in everything I think. Lucretius will always be with my thoughts.

Index